A DOVE
IN THE NIGHT

by

Mark E. Pulsifer

May 3, 2002

Rob,

May God continue
to bless you and
your family.

Mark

This memoir is a true account of selected events from my life. The only changes are the names of people other than myself out of respect for their privacy.

Scripture taken from the HOLY BIBLE, NEW INTERNATIONAL VERSION. Copyright 1973, 1978, 1984 by International Bible Society. Used by permission Of Zondervan Publishing House. All rights reserved.

The "NIV" and "New International Version" trademarks are registered in the United States Patent and Trademark Office by International Bible Society. Use of either trademark requires the permission of International Bible Society.

All quotes from the Tao Te Ching are from LAO TSU: TAO TE CHING, A New Translation by Gia-Fu Feng and Jane English. Copyright 1972 by Gia-fu Feng and Jane English. Vintage Books Edition, September 1972. Vintage Books, a division of Random House. All rights reserved.

ISBN:

This book is dedicated to everyone who has ever wondered

who or what God may be,

and if He really cares about you and me.

TABLE OF CONTENTS

Acknowledgements

The following people are very busy with their own lives and projects. Yet each person, in their own way, made time for me, sharing in my enthusiasm for this important project. Thanks to their help, A Dove In The Night is now a book for others to read and enjoy. Thank you: Andy, Brett and Vanessa, Fr. Brennan, Doris, and Pablo.

Chicago, Illinois   Mark E. Pulsifer
December 2001

Introduction

A Dove In The Night shares a selection of stories from my life so far, written exactly as events occurred. Like most other people, I have had, and still do, my share of difficulties and challenges. At times, my life experiences are so demanding that the only way to survive, after doing all that I need to do, is to surrender completely to God, trusting Him. On another level, the following stories share glimpses of the larger, fantastic universe(s) in which our world is nested but of which we are often only dimly aware.

I have grown and continue to grow out of who I thought I was based on how others treated me, combined with my lack of self-love and knowledge. As that person, I became the cause of much of my own suffering as well as, at times, causing suffering in other people. Living within the Father of all spirits' friendship has helped me develop a healthy love, an honest knowledge, and a gentle but firm discipline and transcendence of myself. As a result, I have become an authentic person living an expanding life. I am inspired with a freedom and a desire to increasingly act in love, kindness, and gentle patience toward others and our planet.

I have reflected deeply upon the selected stories included here. My perspective is tempered by numerous, wide-ranging, expanded reality experiences of other people over a wide period of time and culture in addition to my own numerous, ongoing experiences. For over 30 years I have studied various spiritualities, religions, psychologies, and cultural histories from around the world in an attempt to better understand God, myself, others, and spiritual experience. My experience and faith have been and continue to be greatly enriched thanks to people, cultures, and religious traditions other than my own. I understand that I am on a great spiritual journey, with most elements of the journey common to many people. Everything I have lived is part of that journey and thus is valuable and useful no matter how painful or pointlessly fun it may have been.

Initially, as I began converting into writing my selected life stories from the 30 year "oral tradition" that developed, I was concerned that readers accept every one of the events in this book as literal. It is how I, as well as others who may have been present, experienced them. However, I have since loosened up. I realize that no one can control how another might read, interpret, and understand events such as the ones I share here. With profound poetic economy, the living God I love and worship is able to touch anyone anywhere at anytime in any way useful, communicating either literally or symbolically or both. To insist upon one over the other foolishly or arrogantly creates a false dichotomy which inhibits the deepest apprehension of who we are, who God is, and what the meaning or purpose of life can be.

The following events or phenomena just happened; inviting, informing, and directing my spiritual growth. I did not seek specific or religiously correct experiences. At some point within each story that follows, I simply trusted God wholeheartedly and then acted as if He is Real and really does care. To His credit, He has been there for me every time I have reached out to Him. The few times He seemed to fail me were proper in retrospect as He is sovereign and not manipulated and He was acting in my best long-term interests, like a loving parent.

I have often said that the problem with Christianity is that it is real. The universe does seem to act and respond, frequently in an overt and personal manner. That "God-response" from the spiritual world has the nature and identity of what is known to be the Holy Spirit or Jesus Christ, though at times it is difficult to discern the difference between the two.

What I hope to do by sharing some of my private life is to inspire others with enough courage and curiosity to listen to the stirrings that may be in their hearts, their thirst for something more, and then to do something positive about it. Please contemplate and wrestle with the truths shared on the following pages, testing them, perhaps working them into your heart, your mind, and your life. I believe that the greatest adventure a person can ever live is that of the discovery, exploration, and enjoyment of friendship with the Divine Spirit. Enjoy!

Chapter 1

The Dove in the Night

My parents usually argued nearly every day that they were together. That is, when my father was not traveling. One night during the Summer of 1971 their arguing was particularly distressing to me. I had the sudden idea of praying to God for His intervention and healing or resolution of my parents' arguing.

I grabbed a blanket, my flashlight, and my Bible. I went out my sister's bedroom window onto the garage roof. Normally her window squeaked fairly loud during the full range of opening it wide. This night, however, was different. The window was completely, significantly silent as I opened it. My sister and I looked at each other in amazement. I walked along the edge of the family room roof, then across the roof of the connected garage to the fence. It was a five foot high wooden fence that my father had built around our pool and patio that connected to the far corner of the garage. I slid down off the roof onto the top of the fence. From there it was an easy hop down to the ground.

I walked down through our backyard and into the fields and woods behind our property. It was a moonlit night so I could easily see where I was walking. Even if it was not moonlit, I would not have used my flashlight. I knew the land and I did not want to be found, at least for the night. For a couple of minutes my dad yelled for me from the patio door. My sister and brother must have told them what I was doing when questioned. However, I refused to return. My mind was made up and focused. I would spend the night in prayer.

I did not know where to go to pray. I prayed to God, asking for guidance. I was walking on a footpath through a meadow in which were scattered various trees and shrubs. The footpath led into a large field.

Moments after walking into the field, I heard a lone bird fly away from next to where I was walking slowly. During the day the field was always busy with birds, yet I only kicked-up one bird. There was no peeping or chirping which is more typical especially when you kick-up a bird in a field. The wincing noises express both the bird's startled surprise and the physical effort of becoming airborne. I only heard the flapping of wings which seemed strange to me. Judging by the level of the sound of the flapping wings, the unseen bird that flew up could not have been a sparrow or similar small bird. Rather, it sounded as if it were the size of at least a pigeon or a duck or a dove. I immediately squatted down to try to see the bird silhouetted against the moonlit horizon but did not see any bird. I didn't see it fly away from where I was walking nor did I see it against the night sky. Had it been a normal bird, I would have seen it. All of these thoughts flashed through my mind in an instant, instinctively. It scared me. I thought about returning home. Yet after a moment, I decided to stay and give God a chance to be with me. I sat down to pray and commune with Him.

Because it was summer there were mosquitos. I covered myself with the blanket and began to read the Bible and to pray. I felt His presence, His tenderness. It was a mysterious softness that soothed and comforted me, renewing and strengthening my inner being, giving me fresh hope and courage. At the same time, I could also sense the intimation of His transcendent infinity like passing in front of a large cavern or standing on the edge of an ocean beach late at night. That is, I sensed a great emptiness, an unseen fullness present yet forever beyond me.

After a while I felt the urge to move on, farther into the field, farther away from home, closer to God. I gathered up my Bible, flashlight, and blanket and began walking slowly again through the moonlit field. The moonlight gave everything a blacklight glow of varying monochromatic tones. It was a beautiful night. There was no breeze, no movement, no other sounds. The entire area was very still. Mixed in with the stars and moon, an occasional jet flew silently high overhead absorbed within its own trajectory.

    I walked another hundred yards through the field, past the corner of the dark and quiet forest that bordered one edge of the meandering field. As I rounded that corner and crossed a small stream I again heard the sudden, intense flapping of wings only. As before, the flapping was clear and singular with no chirping or peeping or other noises. Again, I did not see any bird although it was nearly bright enough to read by the moonlight.

    This second time of hearing a bird fly away without being seen made me happy. I felt that God was purposefully communicating with me specifically through His Holy Spirit, a white dove. I stopped the moment the bird flew away for the second time. I figured that spot was where God wanted me to spend the night to pray to Him and to be with Him. I curled up inside my blanket, reading and praying. I eventually fell asleep.

    The next morning was a Saturday morning. I walked home to have breakfast. My parents were calmer that morning and did not fight for a while after that night. I was still amazed and thrilled by the communion I had enjoyed with God the night before. Our friendship was really beginning to develop.

SURVIVING MY YOUTH

THE THORN OF HOPE

TO HAVE A DREAM OR TO PURSUE A VISION
IS TO ENTERTAIN HOPE.

YET HOPE, OFT TIMES, IS A DISCONCERTING QUEST
DEEP WITHIN MY CHEST.

THE PHANTOM OF FULFILLMENT, HOPE IS AS THE
WIND -
TO BE FELT BUT NOT SEEN.

WHY MUST I ENDURE SUCH PAIN WAITING, PERHAPS
IN VAIN,
FOR IT TO COME OF AGE?

I RUN OVER HILL AND THROUGH BOG, DOWN BROKEN
GLASS PATHS AND FLOWERING MEADOWS
IN PURSUIT OF MY VISION AND MY DREAM.

HOPE WILL NOT LET ME REST. IT WILL NOT GRANT ME
PEACE FOR IT WHISPERS TO MY HEART.

THAT MY DREAMS AND VISIONS
CAN BE TRUE
IF I BUT PURSUE THEM.

Chapter 2

My Early Years

I was born on January 5, 1958, to a computer salesman and a former registered nurse in Charleston, West Virginia. We moved frequently. My father was on the rise through the sales ranks into management for a major corporation. My sister and brother were both born in Massachusetts while we lived in a suburb of Boston. My father was originally from the Boston area while my mother was from Cleveland, Ohio.

The most distinguishing characteristic of my childhood was the violent physical and psychological abuse my parents gave me, my sister, and my brother. The abuse, both physical and psychological, was unpredictable, angry, and often explosive. Each day had its own little cruelties and meanness that both parents often perpetuated, my father by far the worst of the two. I was abused in this manner nearly everyday of my life for my first 18 1/2 years. The psychological abuse continued for several years beyond until I grew and healed enough to leave the dance.

Yet, despite the terrible childhood I suffered through, I am thankful to my parents for certain important things that will always be a part of my life, of who I am. Number one would be the genetic inheritance that I received from them. I am glad to be who I am with all of my gifts, talents, and abilities. I am grateful to my parents, especially my mother, for having planted the seeds of faith and curiosity in me, and to an extent, nurturing the same. Another thing for which I am thankful is my involvement in the Indian Guides and the Boy Scouts thanks to my father. The three week backpacking trip to Utah in 1972 imprinted my spirit. I am glad my parents took me skiing as a kid. I loved it. I have always appreciated all of the books and magazines that were in our home during my childhood. I developed a great appetite for reading and have learned a lot because of it. I am also thankful to my mother for never giving up on me or my brother and sister during our teenage rebellion years. The qualities that were codependent or irritating in her as I grew into adulthood were strategically salvific during those dark years. Other parents might have given up but she was too concerned and too stubborn to do so.

Sadly, my experience is no different from what many other people experience as children or adults. Every family is like a group of musicians, each playing their part. Few, if any, families are ever perfectly in tune, at least for more than a few notes. Others seem committed to playing only funeral dirges. Few families seem to exist within healthy, loving marriages though most of us wish for the same. To paraphrase Tolstoy, though each dysfunctional family is tragic in it's own way, the tragedy is not uncommon. The greater tragedy is that this disharmony continues generation after generation all over the world, with no end in sight. We are all at least a little out of tune until we truly begin to heal spiritually, emotionally, and mentally. That is, until we restore proper relationship with ourselves and our Creator (these two primary relationships are interdependent), with other people, and with our planet. This is true and inescapable because we only exist in context to relationship to other things, including God the Father. Nothing exists in isolation, independent of everything or anything else.

Combined with the violence in my house, certain kids attacked and fought me. It happened in my neighborhood, at the school bus stop, and at schools in Ohio, California, and Illinois. I did not have the inner resources to hit back. I wish I did because that would probably have put a quick end to much of the abuse outside of my home. My life was a miserable life of near-constant suffering, pain, tears, and anguish punctuated by brief periods of acting out or anger. Sometimes I would push the normal experimentation or mischeviousness that all kids engage in a step further.

Adding to all the violence and turmoil in my home and in the neighborhood, the cultural backdrop of my youth was the violent, tumultuous decade of the 1960s followed by the laissez-faire 70's. There were beatings in my house and beatings in the Hough Street riots of Cleveland, Ohio and in other cities around the world. Moving from Ohio to California to Illinois within two and one half years was traumatic. The Vietnam War was on the news every night with body counts and scenes of carnage while my mother prepared the evening meal. There were assassinations. Hippies and the counter culture were attacking the mores of society. It seemed that many people became unclear as to what is truly right and wrong. Many began experimenting. They rejected mindless social conformity and the wisdom of the past regarding standards for behavior, thinking those perceived limits could be dropped without detrimental effects. Obviously some standards were false or cultural while other mores are based on centuries of cultural, biological, and spiritual wisdom. Everything seemed fluid, up for grabs. My whole world was unstable, violent, and under attack by violent and confused people. It was extremely unsettling for me.

All the abuse dumped on me created a deep self-hatred and very low to non-existent self-esteem. I developed a deeply embedded pattern for self-destruction that plagued me for the first 19 1/2 years of my life. Beyond that, more subtle patterns of self-defeating behavior plagued me until my early 30s. These internalized negative patterns affected my scholastic efforts and at times, my work too. If I was doing some task very well or about to succeed in a project, a split or duality would emerge inside me pushing me to cease activity so that I would not finish the project or would not succeed. As I began to fight this stupid internal programming, I really had to fight hard against my own inertia; a deeply embedded program to fail myself. It was a part of me however unwanted it was. It was like trying to scratch the middle of my back by myself. It is hard to do.

I found solace in nature. I practically lived outside in the woods, streams, and fields surrounding my home in Ohio.

Tragically, a major housing development put in all around my house ruined the surrounding beauty. Bulldozer operators brainlessly destroyed trees I knew and loved. When I was nine years old, I did save a large, three-trunk oak tree by going out to the bulldozer driver and begging him not to kill the tree. He insisted that he had to take it down. I walked away with my chin on my chest crying. He paused in his enthusiastic orgy of destruction. Maybe he had kids of his own or maybe he just felt bad. A few moments later when my mother walked out to him, she was able to persuade him not to continue his perverse entertainment. To this day that tree still stands between our former back yard and the house built behind it. I will always be grateful to my mother for helping me save that tree. Other times I engaged in eco-terrorism before I even knew what to call it. I was just defending something sacred to me, that's all.

My grandparents and my mother's sister and brother-in-law helped "save" us kids, providing an alternative to the violent, dysfunctional behavior in my family's house by being involved with us. My grandfather was more of a good father to me than my own dad was. Grandpa would take my brother, my cousin, and me camping, hunting, and fishing. My grandparents also took me on cross-country trips to places such as Florida. Those are very good memories.

Early in my life, when I was 5 or 6 years old, I remember standing in front of my toy chalkboard in the basement of our house in Ohio. I remember thinking of my father and his father and how the "badness" passed down from generation to generation to me. I remember thinking, kind of praying to no one or nothing in particular, that I wanted to stop it, to break free. I also thought that when I grew up I would move far away from home and would not write or communicate with my family.

In 1969 my father presented us with the choice of either moving to Germany or to California for his job. If we moved to Germany it would be for one year only whereas California was to be indefinite. I wanted to move to Germany but the decision was made to move to California instead. By August 1969 we had moved to Saratoga, located 50 miles or so south of San Francisco. Us kids were out of our heads with excitement looking at palm trees up close for the first time in our lives.

Saratoga was a fascinating and fun place to live. There were coast range foothills one half mile west, at the end of our street. In the summer and early fall we learned to go "sledding" on the dry grass hills using cardboard instead of using regular sleds on snow covered hills. Although the ride was rougher than snow, which made for hard wipeouts, we never got seriously hurt. My brother, sister, and I quickly learned the hard way that the biggest kid needs to sit in front, otherwise while flying down the hillside the cardboard sled will spin around until the heaviest kid was going first with the lighter weighted kids following. We spun around and went backwards down the hill a couple times. It was a short learning curve regarding that aspect of cardboard sledding. All in all, it was a lot of fun.

We learned from other kids how to ride our bicycles up streets that had steep inclines. The way to do it is to tack back and forth like a sailboat in a headwind, weaving to the top. Other fun discoveries were "frozen Cokes" (when slurpies were first available) at a store on the main downtown street, Japanese gardens, and dried fruits from nearby orchards. Being in the Boy Scouts was great because the camping trips in California were really exciting. We would go to the Sierra Nevadas or to the Pacific Ocean and other great places. We also had a swimming pool in our back yard. I have always loved to swim so having a pool just outside our living room and bedrooms was fantastic! I could not spend enough time in that pool. Being in California, I was able to swim at least seven months out of the year.

Sadly though, the abuse continued. In many ways it intensified because there were no family members nor family friends nearby. We became more isolated than previously. Our time in California was the beginning of serious problems with school and classmates for me. Somehow other troubled kids found me.

Partly I suppose it was because I was a wise guy and partly because I was the "new kid". I firmly believe that most of my horrible suffering outside my home could have been avoided if I had better parental support and if I had the confidence and courage to stand up for myself, making a few noses bloody as necessary. People are surprising. Some people will not give another person any respect unless the "target" person shoves back or hits back, whether with words or fists or both. Once the "target" person has done that, the cowardly bullies usually back off and grant you respect and leave you alone. That's an interesting contradiction if you are trying to follow Christ and to practice love, peace, and patience with other people, regardless of the dimness or brightness of their consciousness.

Across the street from the bottom of our favorite cardboard sliding hill stood a small but very interesting church building. It was a Russian Orthodox church. One day I walked across the street to learn more about the church. The priest who lived there befriended me. I remember talking with him a least a few times, although I no longer recall the specifics of our conversations. What I do remember is his kindness and gentleness. He gave me a copy of a Gideon's New Testament and Psalms that I still have and use. I was only 12 years old but the deep stirrings of my search for union with God and Jesus Christ had begun in earnest. I was awakening to an intense thirst for God. I look forward to meeting the priest again someday to thank him for his kindness, patience, and friendship that he shared with me. In my world of turmoil and violence, it was good to be friends with a good person who was totally outside my daily context. Being kind to others, especially children, is very powerful in positive ways we barely understand.

In the summer of 1970 my family learned that, once again, we needed to move as my father accepted a major promotion. By early September 1970 we settled into a new home in Barrington, Illinois, a suburb located approximately 35 miles northwest of Chicago.

Chapter 3

Teen Years

When I was 12 or 13 years old I began praying for wisdom. For many years I had the desire to control myself, to have an ordered self. It was the same as what I now understand as being spiritually centered. I knew that if I possessed wisdom I would be better able to achieve my desire to be healed, free from my life and self as they were. I also hoped to know others better so I could maybe avoid being hurt by them. Wisdom is that knowledge and way of living that creates proper relationship with ourselves; with others; with the world and how it "works"; and with God. There is great power in wisdom. I knew that even as a 12 or 13 year old, and I wanted some. I figured that if King Solomon could pray to God for it and obtain it, then I should be able to do so too.

I began reading my Bible more. I also began to memorize certain quotations and sayings from various cultures and people that expressed wisdom. I began observing myself, becoming very self-conscious, developing the ability to observe myself as a third person while thinking, acting, or talking. I also began to scrutinize other people too. One early example was my observation of how certain people create rules or patterns of interaction because they possess a lie or have an untenable position or are simply insecure but refuse to admit it and grow out of it. I vowed that if someone else had a better idea or was more correct, I would immediately drop my position and adopt the better one. In this way I could never ultimately be wrong nor would I waste time and energy creating little patterns of lies or "game rules" to avoid having to admit error or insecurity, living in fear waiting to be exposed. You either live in truth or you spend a lot of time and energy creating defenses against it.

During the same period that I began to seek out wisdom, I

was called inward as many adolescents are. I spent hours in my room thinking, reading, listening to music, or building models. Besides my bedroom, my other favorite place was to be alone outdoors, walking through fields or sitting hidden on the edge of a lake, watching the eco-community.

During those times it often felt like I was on a guided tour through various thoughts. I wondered how big is God? How big is big? What is eternity like? Is it static or dynamic? What is the underlying logic or force that holds our universe together? How is reality (time and space) structured? What is time? Is there only one Christ? What is Christ saving us from? Do we need to be saved? If there are other worlds in our universe, do they experience sin too? That is, do those beings suffer from spiritual alienation and entropy as do we? Does a Christ need to appear in those worlds to save those beings too? Does God have realities or universes of which we are totally unaware of? Does Jesus Christ have a similar role in those unknown universes? How might we be sinless in eternity and still retain our original identities or personalities? If Christianity teaches what Reality is all about, what value or weight do I give to all the alternative explanations of what Reality is and how it is structured, especially when the non-Christian teaching may provide an accurate truth or insight that the Christian tradition doesn't address clearly or even missed? I refused to accept simple or dogmatic answers from Christianity or from any other belief system or philosophy.

I would sometimes discuss these questions with the priests at my church or with other adults. Unfortunately, it usually seemed to me that most of the adults I talked with had not asked those types of questions for years, if ever. I never really got any good answers or, in the rare instance that I did, I usually was not ready to accept the answer, at least without testing it. I needed to wrestle with the mysteries of life, to discover truth and make it my own.

I first learned about astrophysics, particle physics, and cosmology during this time in my life. I learned of the quest for a unified field theory that could integrate the theory of relativity, gravity, magnetism, quantum mechanics, wave theory, and electricity. The idea of a unified field theory appealed to me as I was on my own quest for the same from a spiritual and philosophic angle.

Through my freshman high school electronics class I met a very interesting and kind electronics teacher who was conducting experiments with magnetic fields in his home workshop. He was interpreting the first few chapters of the book of Ezekiel literally, believing the being described in those chapters to be a UFO. Although I never saw it happen, it was rumored that his balsa wood and copper wire models had floated and moved magnetically. Coincidentally, the book Chariots of the Gods was published around this time (the early 1970s). Although the author and his book were later questioned by some people as being suspect regarding the rigorousness of research methods and certain conclusions, it was a very provocative book for a year or two after it was first published. Among other postulations, the book argued that UFO encounters were the source of various Biblical experiences. Knowing Mr. Lager and reading the book added to my search for Truth, for God, and for a more complete and less distorted understanding of our world and of myself.

At this same time that my mind and life were expanding greatly, discovering new things almost daily, I began to think a lot about suicide. It began in Spring 1970 while we still lived in California. The first six months of 1970 were a horrible and difficult time for me. I developed a school phobia. For a time, I took a placebo prescribed by our family doctor to calm me down each morning. I was filled with paralyzing fear. After a while I guessed that the little red pills were inert so I stopped taking them. The anxiety, fear, and tension that gripped me daily before and often during school was pure hell. To this day I remain uncertain how I survived that year 1969 - 1970. I remember sitting at my bedroom desk praying a lot or falling asleep praying nearly every night. My mother hung a plaque that had the

Serenity Prayer printed on it in my room. I memorized it within minutes, clinging to it for dear life like a stranded sailor clinging to a scrap of wood drifting in an endless sea.

Shortly after moving to Lake Barrington, Illinois the destructive social abuse and ostracism by other kids started up again. Of course, the abuse and violence within my family never ceased. Things were going from bad to worse for my sister, brother, and I. In general, this time of my life (12 - 19 1/2 years old) was the darkest, most difficult time I have had to live. I could no longer tolerate the abuse, the pain, the terror. Suicide continued to be a possible solution for myself that would also punish my parents. I wanted to emotionally stab them in their hearts as payback for all of the pain they were giving me as much as wanting to end my suffering. But I wasn't certain I wanted to do it, it seemed too permanent of a solution. Instead, I lived with a deepening depression and self-hatred as I tried to make up my mind about what to do. Then I thought of it. I had the answer. I knew what I could do communicate my pain to them without having to kill myself. I would try drugs, the big taboo.

I first smoked marihuana in April or May 1972, shortly before the end of my freshman year in high school. It was in a friend's backyard, sleeping outside with a couple of buddies. All of us knew each other from our membership in the Civil Air Patrol. I was 14 years old. I got stoned the very first time I smoked it. Dave had pot but Tim and Charlie did not know it, especially because they did not use drugs. Dave and I were by ourselves for a while so I had the chance to smoke with him. Shortly after this, the four of us slipped out of Tim's backyard to go bowling nearby.

Airballs and gutterballs were hysterically funny to me. Dave and I couldn't stop laughing. Charlie and Tim had no idea what our problem was. Our behavior irritated them. We bowled only one game. It was during the car ride back to Tim's house that I really noticed interesting changes and distortions in my awareness.

16

After that first high, I wanted to experience it again. Although my initial reason for trying drugs was to rebel, I became fascinated by the changes in normal waking consciousness that psychedelic drugs such as marihuana, LSD, mescaline, and others produce. Among the variety of experiences psychedelics give a person, they open people up to the spiritual world. I wanted to explore the spiritual world as much as possible to find greater intimacy with God, to get control of my painful life so I could change it. I also simply wanted to explore the nature of consciousness and how it interacts with reality. Psychedelic experiences added dozens of questions to my already long list of questions about reality. They became my rabbit hole to Wonderland.

I continued to read the Bible and never stopped praying to and questioning Christ. However, in complement to taking drugs experimentally, I began reading a wide range of books on religion, spirituality, altered states of consciousness, and psychedelic drugs. I partially read the trilogy by Carlos Casteneda about an Indian sorcerer named Don Juan. Becoming a "man of knowledge" was very enticing to me. Aldous Huxley's book The Doors of Perception was a fascinating account of his first experience with mescaline. Of course, I then wanted to try it and eventually did. The Varieties of Religious Experience, written by William James over 100 years ago, had a passage regarding altered consciousness through nitrous oxide, commonly known as laughing gas. Shortly after I read about it, I had some for a tooth extraction at an oral surgeon's office in Barrington. It was a strange and wondrous experience. Teilhard de Chardin, a Jesuit priest and a paleontologist, spoke of an evolutionary, progressive redemption through Christ, a sort of process theology wherein Creation evolves, becoming more divinized in Christ with humanity being the first fruits as is written in the New Testament.. I also discovered the Trappist monk, Thomas Merton, reading his book Seeds of Contemplation. Krishnamurti and Dr. Andrew Weil also provided provocative ideas for my thoughts. Books by Timothy

Leary and Richard Alpert a.k.a. Babba Ram Dass became guide-books for my experiments in awareness.

I was also learning about and "trying on" different religions such as Hinduism, Buddhism, and a brief look at Mormonism. I conducted thought, logic, and perception experiments. I would try to see and understand the world through the teachings or perspectives of various religions or philosophies to see how well each one explained life and our relationship with the ground of all being, whether known as God the Father or the Void or another concept.

Another set of questions that really bothered me centered on my growing ability to know things before they would happen in this world, commonly known as precognition. I discovered that taking drugs usually heightened or enhanced my pre-existing psychic gifts. I began to take drugs to conduct thought experiments of precognition with varying degrees of success. The results were frequently provocative or troubling as well as entertaining. How can events or even we be real if somehow things exist before they manifest in our world "RIGHT NOW"? What then is really real? I tested or compared various religions, philosophies, and teachings in light of the questions and thought experiments that I was exploring. Various ideas or tenets were tried or briefly adopted to compare, mix, and contrast how successful each was (is) in explaining or accounting for events that are anomalies to our daily normal consciousness or experience of commonly accepted reality.

I kept some ideas and discarded others as I continued my search for truth, peace, healing, and union with God. I was not ready to accept mystery, or at least other people's boundaries for mystery. I continued asking, exploring, searching on my own. As mentioned previously, I wanted to find the one explanation that could tie together all of Reality from economics to sociology to mathematics to astronomy to spiritual experiences to physics. All knowledge is related or a part of the Whole. I was searching for a unified field theory of everything that is, if possible. However, the Whole seems to be far more complex and dynamic than anyone living in this world is even capable of wondering about.

Sadly, I chose to continue experimenting and playing with drugs during my teenage years of 14 - 19 1/2 years old. It was my naive hope to produce a permanent change or evolution in my consciousness and being through drugs. I thought and hoped that if I took enough over a period of time and made related changes in my thought patterns, I could achieve a breakthrough. I needed a change from my life as it was.

However, instead of effecting a permanent shift in my awareness, my pot smoking, like a tick or a thorn under my skin, became a pernicious habit that was very difficult to get rid of. It interfered with my developing relationship with God as well as my school work. I know at times I really tested God's patience, but always experienced His love and forgiveness. Certainly, without God's help, I would not have survived and healed from this period of my life.

Chapter 4

Near Death Experiences

Most people can recount one, two, or perhaps three times in their life when they were inexplicably saved from death or very serious injury. The "saving" is always wondrous and unexpected. Typically it is just as sudden as the serious, threatening circumstances that almost caused the death or horrible injury. Personally, I can recount dozens of near misses with death or disaster. It has long been at the point where I believe that I am protected. I expect to be saved from serious injury or death. However, I no longer consciously abuse this gift by engaging in foolish or dangerous behaviors and stunts. I have no doubt Who or What provides this gift of life and health to me. It is God the Father, Creator of All Worlds. Who am I that Thou art mindful of me? Who is anyone else that Thou art mindful of them? Who are You that You care about us?

Divine protection did not become openly apparent to me until I was a teenager. Much of it arose out of the death wish that I developed due to all the negativity beaten into me by the world. Before being forever removed from me when I was 19 years old, that death wish peaked during my teen years. The long list of miraculous "saves" begins when I was about 14 years old. As impressive as many of the stories are that I could share with you, there are three situations that occurred involving my enduro motorcycle (dirtbike) that stand out clearly as being supernatural.

I got my enduro motorcycle when I was 17 years old. All of my friends had dirt bikes too so I had several riding partners. It was a Yamaha 100cc, smaller than most of my friends' bikes but good enough for being wild and crazy. I rode that motorcycle even more recklessly than the way I tended to drive cars. I recognized only two speeds: stopped and full throttle. I would routinely go as fast as I could without wiping out. I did read and practice racing techniques such as braking before entering curves, finding the "berm", playing the slide, and so forth. These things saved me from accident and injury many times. However, there were other times when all the knowledge, preparation, and bravado were insufficient. This is where God intervened directly.

The first openly divine save happened on the day that I went to visit a friend a few miles away. I was in our garage preparing to ride my bike. I checked the oil and gasoline levels. The tires looked OK, no flats from the previous day of trail riding. My brake light and headlamp were in working order. I was not planning to wear my helmet. I just wanted to wear my sunglasses. But a voice with a strong, unseen presence told me to wear the helmet that day. It was as if someone put their finger on my sternum and pressed, "Wear your helmet." At first, I resisted the command. I tried to ignore whoever it was that was telling me to wear my helmet. However, after a moment I relented and wore the helmet. After I decided to obey the unseen someone in my garage by wearing my helmet, I had to decide whether to snap on a plastic duckbill or the acrylic bubble face shield onto my helmet. I decided upon the bubble for no particular reason.

I made it over to Bob's house safely without incident. We goofed around for a couple of hours, then I left to do other things because he had to run an errand with his mother. I said good-bye, put my helmet on, and started the bike. I took off like a rocket down his driveway, popping a wheelie (when the front tire lifts off the ground due to engine torque). I was showing off. I planned to execute a flat track racing slide from the driveway onto the private street that provided access to his home. Both the driveway and the private street were gravel so it was possible to do but you have to be going fast enough to slide around the corner. Approaching the end of his driveway, I began my "flat track" slide onto the gravel drive. I was traveling about 25-30 miles per hour. Suddenly the motorcycle slipped out from underneath me. Falling quickly, my face bounced hard off the handle bars. The force of the impact would have smashed my face on the crossbar of the handle bars. Bob and his mother witnessed my moment of embarrassment. I felt foolish but I was uninjured. I had no neck or facial injuries. It was then that I remembered with thanksgiving and gratitude the firm urging to wear my helmet that Someone had given me in my garage a couple of hours earlier.

The second amazing, divine intervention that preserved me while riding my motorcycle happened when I raced down a cul-de-sac, competing with my friend Todd to see who would get to the trailhead first. The road wound back from Route 59 in a shape similar to an elongated letter "S". Because Todd had a slight lead on me, I resorted to cutting across the front lawns of the homes around which the road curved. I was trying to take a line through the "S" like the line through a dollar sign. It was working because I was pulling slightly ahead of Todd. I shot diagonally across the street to cut through the second house's yard. Todd had wisely stayed on the street to race me.

The owners of that second house had laid a pole next to their driveway. I suppose it was for some type of decorative edging. Perhaps it was there due their inability to back up in a straight line combined with a fervent desire to protect their carefully manicured lawn. I don't know. It certainly was not a welcome sight. It was the type of pole used for telephone wires, about 12 inches in diameter and round. They had buried it such that half of the pole was below ground, leaving six rounded inches sticking above the ground. Shortly before I drove into their yard, I glanced down at my speedometer. I was going 50 mph. I looked back up in the direction that I was traveling only to see the half-submerged telephone pole. I was going too fast to power steer my bike back onto the road and I did not have enough time to stop before hitting it. So I did the best thing that I could think of. I stood up on the foot pegs, hanging my rear-end as far back as possible. I figured that when I hit the half-submerged phone pole, I would be catapulted free of the motorcycle instead of doing a cartwheel with it. I did not want to be suddenly per-

23

forming gymnastics with the motorcycle as my partner. That could hurt me.

I remember hitting it. I felt the impact. I then blacked out for a moment. When I became conscious again, I was looking at the ground as it came toward me in slow motion. I thought my feet were on the foot pegs so I was trying to pull the front end of the bike up to land on the rear wheel first. Unfortunately, the ground got in the way. I hit it hard. Dazed, I sat up on the other side of the front lawn, 40 or 50 feet from the pole next to the driveway. I was sitting in the direction that I had been traveling. I slowly looked around. My bike was behind me, about 10 - 15 feet away. I took my helmet off. The duckbill visor was missing. It was lying on the lawn a few feet away. Todd stopped and turned around.

"Hey! Are you all right?"

"Ya. I'm OK but my leg is hurting," I said.

My right inner thigh muscle was hurting. Apparently I strained it during my wipe-out. I didn't notice the shallow 7-inch gash on my left forearm until I got home 15 minutes later. Fortunately it did not require stitches.

Inside the house that had the telephone pole next to the driveway I could hear the family, their evening dinner sounds filtering out through their front screen door. I was angry with them because I had nearly died on their front lawn and they were completely oblivious. Why did they have that stupid phone pole lying next to their driveway? Didn't they know how to back a car up? At the moment I was not acknowledging that I had everything to do with my accident. I stood up, retrieved the plastic duckbill, and snapped it back onto my helmet. I then limped over to my bike and kick-started it after a couple of tries. The impact left a nice 8-inch divot in the middle of their lawn. Seeing it made me feel better. I felt they deserved it. It was my way of saying "thanks for telephone pole."

When I rode out to the street, Todd spoke first as we headed slowly toward the trailhead at the end of the cul-de-sac.

"I wasn't going to stop because I figured that you would be killed."

"What do you mean?" I asked. "I was trying to pull up the front end to land rear wheel first to ride it out. But I don't remember anything right after I hit the phone pole."

Todd laughed.

"When you hit the pole, you shot up, over, and across the house's front yard. You went higher than their roof! You were holding on upside down. Your feet were straight up in the air. There was a lady walking her dog and when she saw you flying through the air, she grabbed her dog and ran into her house," Todd laughed again. I laughed too.

"When you hit the ground, you were still upside down."

The miracle is that my 1/4 inch thick, slippery smooth, plastic duckbill that snaps onto my helmet had amazingly lined up perfectly parallel to the 1/2-inch round chromed cross bar of the handle bars. It broke my fall, deflecting the force of falling 20+ feet back to earth face first. Had that not occurred, my face and everything behind it would have smashed onto and past the cross bar, killing me. I would have left more than a divot on that front lawn. Apart from the two minor injuries mentioned above, I had no neck injuries nor any other problem. My strained leg muscles healed within a week or so. The gash on my left forearm healed without infection or scarring.

Again, God had saved me directly. Based upon the accident facts, there was no reason I should have lived, especially without crippling injury, other than Divine protection. I was very grateful to be alive and well. Also, my motorcycle survived the fall fairly well. It was still under warranty so the little damage that it sustained, an unseated oil pump in the bottom of the engine block, was easily repaired at no cost to me. It was viewed as being a factory defect in the engine.

The third event involving Divine protection did not protect me immediately from injury. In the long run, however, the injury probably saved my life. After this next accident that I am about to describe, my parents made me sell the motorcycle. After that, there was no more kamikaze bike riding. The accident happened on a Saturday in July 1975. I know this because I had right knee surgery on August 14, 1975, to repair the damage done in July.

On that fateful Saturday, my friend Tony and I were riding around together. He had a Kawasaki 125. Late in the morning he stopped at his home for lunch. We agreed to meet again in about 45 minutes. I decided to spend the waiting time riding around the town of Barrington where he lived.

Suddenly, as I was leaving the alley driveway next to his house, I had a vision. It was as if someone pulled a movie screen down over the lens of my consciousness, similar to an in-flight movie on a passenger jet. It was very detailed, yet like a dream, it lasted only a few seconds as I drove down the street toward the stop sign at Lake Cook Road.

In the vision I saw myself riding my motorcycle and rear-ending a car, hurting one of my legs. Then, starting at the same beginning in the vision, I saw myself just riding along and falling over, again hurting one of my legs. I understood that I had to make a choice. Which scenario did I want? Which one did I prefer? It was as compelling as the time I was told to wear a helmet. The vision and the choice demanded bothered me. After a moment of thought, I very clearly chose to fall over and get hurt without a car being involved. I never liked the possibility of cars being involved in a motorcycle accident because either the car or the hysterical reaction of the driver would make any injury and situation worse. I very clearly preferred that if I was going to get hurt, it should be by myself. The vision left me. The vision was completely unsought and unexpected. It troubled me for several minutes, sticking to me with conviction or inevitability. However, I was finally able to push it out of my mind, forgetting it.

I met up with Tony in a bit and we eventually made our way out to an old quarry north of Island Lake to do some dirt riding, jumping, hill climbing, or whatever with our motorcycles. We were riding along the rim of the quarry, trying to figure out how to get down into it. Tony was in the lead as we traveled at walking speed along the rim. He paused briefly, just after a little dip in the trail we were on. I tried to stop but somehow my slow reaction combined with the change in ground levels caused me to bump into Tony's rear tire. I was only going 3 miles per hour at most but it was sufficient to knock Tony over his handle bars because he was standing up on the foot pegs, scouting around. I fell over and ripped my right leg up sideways so that my foot nearly touched my shoulder. The vision was fulfilled. God's will came to pass.

A couple weeks later I had right knee surgery to repair torn ligaments and cartilage. The motorcycle was sold. In the years since then, although I have ridden other friends' bikes over the years, I have not yet bought another one for myself. Perhaps someday I will. However, I will seriously pray about it first. I will be ready for that day should it ever come for I am no longer self-destructive nor a kamikaze driver.

I have always known that it was God who warned me. What is interesting, though, is that I can share this story with six different people and get six different explanations. It was God; it was an angel; it was Jesus; it was the Holy Spirit; it was a spirit guide; or it was some saint or perhaps even Mary who warned me and protected me. Who knows? All six answers may be correct one way or another. However, I have never been willing to impose a forced or dogmatic, cliched understanding or distinction on the vision and the accident.

I was protected, given a choice. I have always given God credit for it. He can figure out who else should share in my gratitude if He enlisted the assistance of a creature such as an angel in giving me the vision. That creature (my guardian angel perhaps?) understands my waiting to personally thank them. That being understands that humanity is involved in a mysterious trans-reality struggle for our hearts and minds; for our wills and lives. It seems to be a cross between a cosmic custody battle, a civil war, and our own neurotic impulses. Misinformation concerning God, spirit guides, the Holy Spirit, and so forth is common. Any heavenly creature who loves God will always point us directly toward Him rather than accept our praise and worship for theirselves. To do less means that the spiritual being is probably struggling with their own rebellious choices, and therefore should not be trusted.

Chapter 5
Crash But No Burn

June 1976 to mid-August, 1977 was the darkest year of my life. It is the year that if I was going to kill myself, it would have been then. The cumulative effect of all my 18-19 years of abuse and negative programming reached a toxicity that nearly finished me off. In June 1976 I graduated from high school. At that point in my life, I had not yet learned personal discipline nor how to plan for the future. Even though I had plans and ideas about how to possibly live my adult life, I had none of the "tools" for attaining those goals. Consequently, I was somewhat directionless. All I really knew was that I needed to desperately escape from my family and my own miserable state of being. But I really did not know how.

I thought that joining the US Navy would be a quick and easy way out and away from my situation. I was very interested in becoming a SEAL. This was long before it attracted the attention of Hollywood. However, two things made me change my mind about enlisting. The first was that my previously injured right knee (from the motorcycle accident and subsequent surgery) was not strong enough to make it through the requisite training. Second, even during peacetime in 1976 there was a 3-4 year waiting list to get into the SEALS. Guys who were enlisted in UDT (Underwater Demolition Team) were re-enlisting, waiting for the opportunity to try out for the SEALs. Getting into the SEALs was very uncertain unless I wanted to be in the Navy for several years and even then there were no guarantees. So I decided not to enlist. Another idea I did not follow through on was to go to college at the University of Alaska in Anchorage. Even though I was accepted, my parents would not pay for it. This was before I knew anything about school loans or grants so I did not go. In hindsight, I recognize that it must have been the mysterious grace of God to not have taken either path. Either choice would have been the wrong thing for me at that time.

What I did do that summer was apply at the last minute to attend Western Illinois University (WIU). I basically chose it because a good friend, Dave, was going to start there in September, 1976. I had no direction, discipline, or plans, so applying to WIU made as good sense to me as any other choice. I went on a two or three week trip to Colorado in early August. Upon my return I learned that WIU had accepted me. I was off to college.

Drugs were prevalent at WIU at that time without having to look too hard for them. I was staying in a room on the 11th floor of Lincoln Dormitory. My roommate liked pot as much as I did so we got along fairly well. He also had a good stereo, which was important. On our dorm floor everybody partied regularly. I attended classes but with the lack of studying, and the marihuana and other drugs, I did not learn nor retain very much. I had a few friends at WIU, including Dave although we tended to be in our own separate worlds and circles of friends. For awhile, I was helping deal marijuana on campus. My supplier and I clicked. He needed someone to help sell pot in the dorms. I needed to subsidize my habits. So it only made sense that I dealt drugs for him. I remember walking past a police car with two pounds of marihuana underneath my coat. I needed to keep my hands in my coat to hold each bag from underneath. I worried that if the cops asked for my college ID, I'd have to take my hands out of my coat to dig my wallet out of my pants pocket, allowing the big plastic bags to fall into plain sight in front of the police officer. That would be embarrassing.

That year on campus a professor was teaching a class entitled, "The Psychology of Consciousness". He used materials from people such as Dr. Charles Tart and Dr. Andrew Weil. I introduced myself and we became friends, drawn together by a mutual interest in the nature and mechanism of human consciousness and how it can be filtered, bent, twisted, changed,

30

manipulated through drugs, fasting, meditating, and so forth. I visited him at his house often to discuss all sorts of things or to smoke pot. I was very lonely, feeling the pain of my "missing father". I have often felt that my earthly father really only sired me, he did not raise me as it seems a true father would. Here finally was someone I could talk to about drugs and consciousness in a nonjudgmental way. We were both searching for truth at it's deepest and most sublime. I wanted to be certain that our friendship would be strong. I threw out my Christianity and adopted more of his beliefs of reincarnation. This fit neatly with my own study and readings on the subject. My (mis)understanding of Hinduism, certain types or styles of meditation, and psychedelics drugs seemed made for each other. At that point in my life, I was searching for God and for ultimate truth through these paths. Adopting reincarnation (and thus denying Christ) was a fairly easy thing to do at that time in my life. However, I never quite accepted that belief completely, it never really sat well with me. But I certainly tried it on, testing it in my thoughts and in my daily life, to assess the veracity and accuracy of that belief.

During that autumn, I witnessed a regressive hypnosis session that the professor performed in front of several other people at an evening meeting in a lodge somewhere just outside of Macomb, Illinois. Witnessing a person allegedly regress hypnotically back into an alleged previous life creates strong cognitive dissonance with your currently held beliefs. It was very provocative, challenging the beliefs and assumptions I had made or been taught about the structure of reality and what it is to be a human being. It also caused me to really question just exactly who or what God is. The net effect was to move farther away from the Christ and the God I used to commune with.

I tripped once a week for 9 or 10 weeks in a row during Fall Term, 1976. That is, I ingested LSD or a similar psychedelic compound once each week, in addition to all of the marihuana and other assorted (sordid) drugs I was taking. I usually took the psychedelic substance with other people. Each "trip" tends to last 7 - 10 hours. A couple of my friends and I would take psychedelics together. The Psychedelic Book of the Tibetan Dead by Drs. Timothy Leary and Richard Alpert (before he became Baba Ram Dass) was a book written to facilitate exploration of the nature and structures of consciousness. We would ingest psychedelics and then read the book, sharing our immediate experiences of ego dissolution, expanded awareness, and so forth. I would examine, disassemble and question all of the assumptions and default parameters of my own mind while under the influence of the drug. In retrospect, it seems that I was attacking my own mind and my own sanity. My deep rage due to my family situation, coupled with honest curiosity about consciousness, propelled me toward self-destruction.

As part of my attempt to achieve a permanently higher awareness and to live closer to God, I believed that I needed to deny all of my feelings. It fit with what I (mis)understood of Hinduism and related belief systems. In retrospect, I was also doing it in a desperate attempt to escape my suffering, to self-medicate through denial and attempted control.

All of these activities increased and deepened my isolation and loneliness. It seemed that I was entirely alone although surrounded by people. I was quickly sinking deeper and deeper into dangerous depression as if falling down a seemingly bottomless undersea rift. Crushing darkness was increasing as I sank in my sea of pain. Waves of despair danced on the surface. By November, 1976 I would often stand at my 11th floor dorm window, wearing headphones listening to music. I would press against the window, playing with the flex in the glass, wondering how hard I'd have to push to 'break on through to the other side'.

My curiosity was impatient and my need for relief desperate, yet I was afraid to do it, to break the glass and plunge to my death. I had the direct sense that just behind the thin veil of space-time sits God the Father. Killing myself would make Him angry. I certainly was not imagining this. My pain and depression were too crushing to play imaginary games with myself. I just knew that it was the wrong thing to do. I contemplated this for several weeks. I did not want to have to stand in front of Him to tell Him that I couldn't handle the life that He gave me. It would be throwing His gift back in His face. Eternity is a long time - the last thing I wanted to do was anger the Transcendent Center of Eternity, the Creator of all that is, the Father of all spirits. That would be going from bad to worse. Rather than commit suicide and rip a permanent, non-repairable hole in the fabric of reality, I postponed it, but I didn't know what to do. I had no hope but somehow managed to limp along despite my intense suffering. I got my break during Christmas Break 1976 - 77.

My mother had been receiving counseling to help her deal with her marriage. It was with a psychiatrist affiliated with a local hospital's psychiatric program. She asked me if I wanted to talk with him to try to get some help for my desperate state. I eagerly said yes. Within a couple of days I visited the doctor. My mother had driven to the appointment with me and waited outside of his office while we talked. He suggested that I could benefit from an in-patient stay in their psychiatric program. He stressed that because I was 18 years old he could not hospitalize me without a court order. But he strongly felt that I needed to be hospitalized for a short course. I said yes because I couldn't think of any better way to get out from under my crushing depression. The doctor made a couple of phone calls, and I was admitted to the hospital across the street within the hour.

Every new arrival to the psychiatric area spends a day or two on the 8th floor, which is the General Psychiatric Ward. Patients are assessed and categorized, then placed into whichever program they need to be in. It was disturbing to be there. The other patients frightened me. Some were really wacko. There was the Darvon Lady, addicted to painkillers. She was kind of nice, somebody's grandmother. The song "Mother's Little Helpers" by the Stones comes to mind. The repeat alcoholic told me that he would successfully kill himself next time rather than fail himself again with drinking or with botched suicide attempts. The depressed police officer had a failing marriage and had seen too much ugliness on the streets of Chicago. It was eating at him like acid corroding metals pipes. There were housewives, teachers, young drug abusers, psychotics, people from all walks of life.

I had a frightening insight. I realized that these people in the hospital were not really that different from anybody else walking on the streets outside the hospital. It was just that the patients' problems had become inconvenient or in the way or no longer able to be hidden, necessitating "treatment". That is, it was really the first time that I realized that many people are sick in their psyches and spirits but that they either had not yet been hospitalized or their sickness somehow aided them in functioning in society and achieving cultural symbols of success. Furthermore, it seemed that a lot of the treatment that the hospital and staff provided was simply adjusting or "fixing" the aberrant aspects of a person's personality or psyche so that when they are discharged from the hospital, they could "fit in" again.

Despite an arrogant confidence in their abilities, a "We know best" attitude, the hospital staff cannot heal anybody, they can only patch patients up. They can not provide or create meaning for me or for anyone else. Each patient really needs to do this. This is the essence of what it is to be human, to feel the pain and joy of existence. This is essential to living your own life, of taking responsibility for your own life, thoughts, actions. Most illnesses involve or provoke a crisis of meaning and values, especially mental illnesses — or they should. No healing is complete until your spirit is healed, restored, reunited with your source Being, the Father of all spirits. I now have the language and understanding to articulately write about the hospital experience and that first major, significant, disturbing insight into the sickness of individuals and societies. But at the time it was very frightening.

In the hospital, wondering how to heal and grow, I realized that I could not mindlessly return to society by just covering up my malaise and depression by "coping" or becoming a good little consumer. Yet I knew that the way I was trying to live was a way of death. It was a disturbing position to be in. I knew that there was only one way for me to survive and heal. Immediately upon my entrance to the hospital, I admitted my wrongdoing to God and began praying again, conversing with my true center, God Almighty. I renewed my prayerful dialogue with Christ. Absolutely, everything I learned while in the hospital programs and everything I let go of was critical, but my renewed relationship with God is what led me into health again. It was strategic.

I was exhausted emotionally and mentally upon my admission and needed something to hold onto while I rested and healed the way a tired swimmer holds onto a buoy while swimming in open water. I wanted the world to stop for awhile. But time waits for no one, so I prayed for float time so I could rest, heal, and develop strength and direction. Fortunately, Jesus was my 'something solid' to cling too as I floated through the deep, dark waters.

I realized that everyday everyone has three basic choices and that we all consciously or unconsciously choose one of the three choices and live them. The choices are: kill yourself, either overtly or simply by choices that lead you away from life; stay where you are; or grow in new life. For me, I hated where I was at but I was not certain how or in what direction I should grow. I reasoned that I can always kill myself tomorrow so I might as well try new growth or new behavior today. Another useful thought that helped keep me going during my two weeks in the hospital's Depression Program was a desire to some day return to Canada to go canoeing. A third useful thought was that I did not want to be defeated by my present circumstances. I was going to be defiant to the end. The fourth strategic thought that really helped me (whether truly accurate or not - my disclaimer for any gardeners who might be reading this book) was that flowers and gardens grow best with some shit mixed in. If it seems that you are getting dumped on with truckload after truckload so that there is a heaping, smelly, mound of dung in your front yard, don't fret.

35

It is just Life urging you to make a bigger garden. In fairness to the hospital and their psychiatric programs, I doubt that I would have survived the crisis if the hospital had not been there for me. I learned or accepted some good things, including the importance of how to talk about the weather and other topics with people. There is an important role for simple conversation or small talk. It is the way we connect with each other in a simple but important way. It helps to create and reaffirm relationships between people and groups. My insistence on being profound all of the time was arrogant. It created an imbalance. My refusal to accept normal social interaction isolated me to the point of harm. But overall, the program had its limits.

Through the above described combination of prayer, repentance, and my four strategic thoughts, I survived. I bounced when I hit bottom. I didn't splat. At the end of the two week inpatient stay, I was discharged to a two week "day hospital" program. It is a program where you attend a full day at the hospital but live at home, commuting back and forth each day. By the end of this four week period, I knew that I was ready to get away from the American psychiatric system and away from all of the other "inmates". I knew what I had done wrong, had corrected it, and thus felt that I had no further need of professional assistance.

My Freudian trained doctor who was agnostic at best and not really a deep thinker, had diagnosed me as being manic-depressive-manic meaning that to him, I only manifested the manic half of that bipolar disease. That is because my first few nights in the hospital I resisted going to bed until I knew I was tired enough to immediately fall asleep in order to bypass the imagery you often "see" when laying in bed. I had taken a lot of LSD and other psychedelics for weeks, attacking my reality constructs, seeing how far I could go and still return to myself. At the hospital I needed to hang around normal waking consciousness and avoid any possible excursions away from it. It was like clinging to a life raft or refusing to enter the water at the beach for fear of being pulled out to sea by riptides and drowning. Thus, I was afraid to fall asleep for a week or two. To the doctor, this was evidence that I was manic, confusing terror with manic energy. His diagnosis was a complete and arrogant misunderstanding of me and of what prompted me to admit myself to the hospital on my own volition in the first place. Nowadays, more enlightened psychiatric knowledge allows for organic mood disorders due to heavy drug usage. This was closer to what was ailing me.

I needed a new muffler but now I was getting a brake job, too. He prescribed lithium. I resisted because I knew he was grossly wrong. But my mother, wanting to help, told me that I could not live with her if I did not obey the good doctor. I had no job, no other income, and needed support and friendship. So I complied. But I only took it for a couple of weeks at most. I hated and resented it. It fuzzed me up like trying to tie shoelaces while wearing mittens and slowed me down like driving a car with its parking brake on. It was a drag on my mental energies, it cut off thoughts or dimmed them. I strongly fought my mother in a battle of will. She realized after awhile that I wasn't taking it anymore. She backed off finally. Of course, the good doctor was very disappointed with me, telling me so.

In conjunction with being told to take lithium, Dr. I.M. Right a.k.a. U.R. Wrong greatly pressured me to attend a weekly evening group therapy program associated with the hospital. I knew that I did not need it and I was tired of being around other patients. They were all scared or angry or inflexible or confused or lost within theirselves in varying combinations. After the initial terrifying shock of suddenly being thrown together with all these different types (to briefly be in the same group) began to wear off, being around the other patients became irritating and a drag. Many of them seemed to be sitting in their little puddles and soiled clothing crying, wallowing, hoping and demanding that someone else come and wipe them off, solve their problems, and live their lives for them. Worse, the staff accommodated them in this, encouraging dependent reliance upon them. Properly employed, this can be an invaluable technique in helping another heal and gain strength. It was just that I was rebounding faster than the staff's therapeutic models allowed.

Thanks to my repentance with God and His forgiving love for me, combined with my realization that what I had been living, doing, thinking to that point was wrong in varying degrees set me on the path to health and freedom. The Holy Spirit was also working in me in ways that I was conscious of, showing me thought patterns and behaviors that were making me ill and out of tune. This was something that the therapeutic models and staff could not account for. Spirituality was not part of the equation, therefore it was ignored as being the critical element of human health, integration, and wholeness.

In the day-hospital program, I had been surrounded by people who did not seem to truly want to change, to flow, to morph. Or they were afraid to try. Instead, they were demanding reality bend, flex, and flow around them. This is guaranteed to cause mental illness if carried too far and for too long. As in the various hospital programs, the demand that the rest of the world flow around "me" is also frequently encountered in daily life with "difficult" or even highly "successful" people in business or at the supermarket or wherever. In the mornings, many people take their young children to daycare then drive to their own adult daycare commonly known as "the office". I didn't want to have to spend more time being around the same types of people in a weekly evening group therapy program. I did not want to remain ill and definitely did not want to remain or become dependent on any programs or pills or anything else except God alone.

Dr. Right again reminded me that because I was now 19 years old (my birthday is in early January), he could not legally force me to attend the weekly evening group therapy. But he knew that I needed it because everyone else needs it. Like a backup singer, my mother jumped in behind him, telling me that if I did not comply I would not be able to live at her house.

It had been our family home until I admitted myself to the hospital. It was at that time that she finally decided to legally separate from and divorce my father. When my dad moved out it was as if bullets were removed from the figurative hand gun that had been constantly pointed at our heads. Immediately a lot of the pressure and stress within my family was gone, or at least within me. But now it was "her house". I was fighting for my health and freedom despite the best efforts of the psychiatric profession and my mother.

I negotiated a compromise with them. I told them that I would go to the group therapy once to check it out. If I decided that I did not need it, I would not continue going and they would not bug me about it. They reluctantly agreed. Dr. Right reminded me that I had been fighting him and resisting his "help" since my initial admittance a month earlier. Thank God I was over 18 years old when I hit bottom. Who knows what would have happened to me if "they" had legal control over me and my life. This will always bother me. I was almost trapped in the American psychiatric gulag. Had I accepted what Dr. Right and the other hospital staff were trying to tell me, I still would not be healed.

I went to the group therapy and support meeting one evening during the week following my successful attendance and completion of the two week day-hospital program. By now it was late January 1977. This first meeting was a trip. There were adults of varying ages and backgrounds who belonged to the group. Many had been attending for years. Others were repeat members. I couldn't believe it. It seemed amazing and sad.

Over the years I have come to truly understand just how difficult life is for most of us walking around on planet earth. It is one of the most truthful insights Buddha ever realized: Life is difficult. I understand and appreciate how difficult it can be for a person to extricate and free him- or herself from a sick family or other corrosive relationships. I personally know how difficult it is to try to develop will power against certain personality flaws or weaknesses. I have lived the pain, shame, and frustration of repeated will-power failures. At times I have run from growth; or have been too tired; too weak; too afraid; or too confused to try new behavior or new growth. But I have fought those battles and I have won. In some of my struggles, it has taken years but I have pressed on until I developed deeper healing and greater self-mastery.

I am not superhuman. Far from it. Rather, I am an ordinary person. My key to survival is that: (1) I have never given up; (2) I literally believe that with God nothing is impossible; (3) that Christ will strengthen me in all things; and (4) I accept response-ability for my life, for who I am, and for who I am becoming. At times I have been very angry with the life and the struggles I have been given; at times I have been very angry with God, and with other people. Many of my problems were directly caused or set in motion by other people around me. But so what. I am the only person who has the right and the power to live my life. No one else can do it for me. So even if I was dealt a bad hand, it is up to me to make it better. I have also recognized that an excellent way to get even with the miserable louts who injured or abused me in various ways is to heal, grow, and blossom spiritually. I evolve while "they" remain stuck within their dysfunctional loops and limits. They cannot escape from their own mess. Think of all the people who have spiritual diaper rash in our world. Importantly, I know that I need the fellowship and assistance of other people to help me become freer, healthier, more myself. Even the Lone Ranger had Tonto. But only I — not even God — can live my life. Only I can make the most critical choices involved in who I am. This is exactly why I healed. I accepted these incontrovertible truths and acted on them.

The people I met in the group seemed to be engaged in group wallowing. The group therapy sessions was their common life raft in a sea of pain, fear, and illness. Worst of all, it seemed that the hospital staff counselor encouraged their dependence upon him, the psychiatric system, and to some extent, upon fellow group members. I have been to a lot of boring and pointless events ranging from corporate staff meetings to blind dates, but those three or four hours in that group session stand out as being the worst. What almost everyone needed was a 'shove out of the nest'; encouragement and empathetic challenge to grab their life with both hands and resume responsibility for living it and for the consequences of their choices. To be wounded or weak is one thing. To remain in that situation for too long is wrong. At some point people need to take responsibility for their lives and stop being a victim, or lazy or making excuses or repeating their sin(s) — the falling short of who they can be. I had nothing in common with the people or the counselor in that group therapy program.

I called the counselor mid-week after that first session to inform him that I did not need to be in his group and that I was not going to go back. He was upset, disappointed, and angry. Worst of all, he was as manipulative as Dr. I.M. Right was. "Keep them in the system. Don't let any of them escape or quit before they have our approval to leave." Of course my father's health insurance was paying for it so there may have been more than one motive behind their great care and concern for me. When I told Mr. Counselor that I was not going to continue attending his group sessions, he laid it on thick. He told me that the people in the group had opened themselves to me. If I did not go back to explain that I was not rejecting them personally, simply that I did not want to be in their group, I would be setting them back therapeutically. I thought that it was nonsense, but at the same time I did not want to add to the group patients' problems. Had I the strength and assertiveness that I now possess, I would have told this counselor where to go and what to do with himself when he got there. But I didn't. Instead, I reluctantly agreed to go to the stupid meeting to say good-bye to complete strangers who seemed pathetic to me.

I arrived at that second meeting a couple of minutes late. I really did not want to be there, so getting there was a struggle of will. When I got to the meeting room in one of the hospital wings, everyone was angry with me. I was either being ignored or treated with rudeness and hostility, depending upon the person. Apparently the very fine hospital staff counselor told the group of my intentions to quit their group. I was only 10 or 15 minutes late and the first part of their therapy sessions was always social mixing prior to the all important assembling of chairs into a circle for therapeutic talking, talking, talking and mutual support. I still do not understand why that counselor told his group that I was going to quit before the meeting even started.

When we all sat down in the circle to talk and share, I was on the receiving end of a barrage of questions. What would I do if I could not handle being alone in the world? How could I handle all of the problems that I was going to have? How could I be confident that I would not have the same toxic reaction to my family situation and everyday problems if I didn't have their support and guidance? They almost talked me out of my decision. But I knew that if I had Jesus Christ, I would succeed. I already knew that I was going to be OK. At last, I spoke up.

"Hey, if I mess up, I can always come back. But right now I don't need to be here."

Even the fine hospital staff counselor was angry with me, expressing contempt and doubt regarding my decision and my ability to never need him or his hospital program ever again. Or perhaps he was going to miss my father's group insurance money. I don't know for certain. After it became clear that I was now an anathema to the group, I said the hell with them and left their meeting early. No one said 'Goodbye" to me as I left.

I have never been back. I have never needed to go back. I will never need to go back because I have learned and grown. My life has changed permanently for the better, and I now know that I can never be defeated unless I give up and quit trying. I can just be temporarily setback or redirected in life but I can never be defeated.

In chapter four of the first book of John in the New Testament, it is written that God is love. If this is true, then it follows that all things in all worlds dwell or exist within love. God as love is transcendent, omniscient, integrative, healing, and life restoring. He calls forth all things into being and sustains them as He wills. Thus, I knew that because I had repented and again turned to God for help, I would be able to do all things necessary for me to grow, heal, and become successful in life (which means more than earning a lot of money). I had faith (hopeful belief) that all things conspire for the good of people who love God. I knew that I would still have pain and struggle. But if God is with me and helping me, I will prevail if I persist in my efforts to heal. And it is true, I have healed. So have countless others who have also relented, repented, and (re)turned to God for assistance, new life, growth, and healing.

I firmly believe that the best and most permanent healing is really a function or consequence of growth in holiness and intimacy with God. We are relational beings. We only exist in relation to others. By turning toward God, the ultimate OTHER, the Source of All Being, we enter into our most primary relationship which then affirms and informs our individual lives. By remaining in relationship with this great OTHER, our Creator, we become blessed with new strengths, abilities, and visions of being and life, enabling and inspiring us to heal, grow, and attain new and greater life including relationships or community with others. The greatest thing that anyone can ever do is to discover and become their true eternal self which can only be discovered in the course of friendship with the Holy Spirit.

NEW LIFE

WOUND

I have a wound that won't heal.

A piece of glass in my shoe.

God is stirring in my soul.

Chapter 6
Season of Emptiness / Sea Change

Even though frequent and earnest prayer with Jesus Christ had delivered me from self-destruction earlier in the year (Crash But No Burn), like most people, my praying gradually subsided in frequency and duration as I healed from my nearly fatal low point. I did not need God now as much as I did a few months earlier. Hollow emptiness seeped in as if my diminishing prayers were a bilge pump that was slowing down. I truly was dead in my spirit.

I drifted back to smoking marihuana. I was also drinking more. I did not do these things with any joy, it was just a natural drift; a self-medication. I was still directionless regarding vocation and what I was to do with my life. Yet I was in no hurry to join the mindless consumer treadmill of a comfortable life in the suburbs. To me that seemed as certain of a death to my spirit as returning to partying again. I was adrift; no rudder; no sails; no compass; and jagged rocks were looming all around.

During Summer 1977 I had a job painting houses with a college crew. It was fun. I always enjoy working and being outside. I had a fun girlfriend as well as a few friends who still lived in the area. I was able to keep myself busy enough so that I did not feel too much pain due to my emptiness. It was precisely at this time in my life that something very curious occurred.

My friend Brad, one of his brothers, and I went to the very first Star Wars film one Sunday afternoon in early July. We saw it at the former Edens Plaza Theaters in Northbrook, Illinois. The relationship between Luke Skywalker and Obi Wan Kanobe captivated me. The spiritual apprenticeship struck a chord in me. I felt a yearning to be like them: developing spiritual warriors. However, I reminded myself that I had nearly destroyed myself in my quest for spiritual knowledge and mastery. I was reluctant to try again.

After the film ended, we exited through the lobby. Suddenly I heard an unseen someone talking to me. All of us have our thinking voice. It is that aspect of consciousness that provides the narration and continuous chatter by which we, in part, think, feel, and act. The voice that spoke to me was immediately alien or separate and distinct from "me", from "my voice". It was similar to wearing a telephone headset talking with someone on the telephone. Their voice is in your head with your voice.

"Why don't you become a man of knowledge?"

"I can't. I don't know how," I replied.

I wanted to say yes but I was scared. My time at WIU and then my trip through the hospital with the months of struggle afterward left deep wounds that were still very fresh. Scars were only just beginning to form.

The phrase "man of knowledge" I understood to mean to be like Don Juan, the protagonist in Carlos Casteneda's trilogy. Don Juan was allegedly a Yaqui Indian sorcerer who was very much at home in the spiritual world or at the intersection of the spiritual and physical worlds. But I knew that the unseen someone wasn't urging me to become a sorcerer. Rather, it was simply that the term "man of knowledge" instantly made sense to me. It was just a matter of good communication. I sensed that it was the Holy Spirit speaking to me.

With reluctant impatience, I "pushed" the unseen someone and their voice away from me. The conversation took place within the span of a few moments while I exited the theater. I said nothing to Brad about it. I felt more alone, lost, and frustrated than before that special conversation. The invitation heightened my despair the way sunlight sharpens dark shadows.

A couple weeks later I was forcing myself to paint a client's house on a Sunday morning. I was the only crew member there. Working on Sundays was not part of the summer house painting job requirement. I was trying to earn some extra money and to prove to myself that I was a hardworking, disciplined person.

However, because my heart was not into painting, I was open to any good excuse that I could accept to quit working that morning. Coincidentally, the house that I was painting was right next door to my girlfriend's parents' home.

Late in the morning Valerie's mother came over to tell me that my mother was stranded at church, her car would not start. Apparently my brother, who went to church with her that morning, was unable to figure out the problem and fix it, whatever it was.

Initially irritated for being called, I quickly realized that I now had an excuse for myself to discontinue painting. I quickly cleaned up, putting the brushes and paint back into the corner of the garage that our client let us use while painting their house. I arrived at St. Michael's within ten minutes of the telephone call. When I got there, I found my mother in Fr. O'Leary's office, chatting with him and a fellow parishioner, Anita Brodke.

"Mark, your brother was able to get the car started afterall," my mother said. "I tried calling you back but you were already on your way here."

Perhaps the engine had been flooded, I wondered. I was no longer needed, but my mood for Sunday house painting had completely vanished. I was glad to be there rather than on a ladder leaning against the side of a house, applying a shade of green that I had dubbed, "Fort Sheridan green" (a putrid, flat, military green).

While my mother talked with Anita, I decided to ask Fr. O'Leary about some of the many nettlesome questions that were chafing my mind and heart. I had spoken with him before and was acquainted with him. Figuring that I had nothing to lose and perhaps a lot to gain, I tested him to see how well he might grapple with my questions about the structure of space-time and what is really real if people can know things routinely before they happen in this world. These recurrent, undeniable expanded reality events, often experienced with my friends while we were all together, were like little pieces of glass in my shoes.

"Hi Father. Hey, I was wondering. Do you mind if I ask you some questions that I've been wondering about?"

"No, go ahead. What are they?" Fr. O'Leary said.

"How can Reality exist before the eternal moment of Now passes through it? How can things exist before they occur in this world?"

As he began to answer these questions, I asked him some others.

"What is real? How does our reality of space-time intersect with the spiritual world? Do you think that our world is suspended within the spiritual world like droplets of water in fog, with NOW vibrating certain space-time droplets in an infinite variety of sets?"

I was hoping that he would be a good person to talk with. Even if I was afraid to go deeper, I was, by nature, on the search anyway. Suddenly Anita interrupted our conversation.

"Father, this boy is a seeker. Send him to Anna! She can help him with his questions."

Immediately, Anita, Fr. O'Leary, and my mother began an animated discussion about whether I could benefit by going to Anna (whomever she was) for spiritual counseling. Abruptly, Fr. O'Leary paused and turned to me.

"Wait a minute. Let's ask him if he wants to meet Anna."

"Who is she?" I asked.

Both Fr. O'Leary and Anita explained that she was a born-again, Charismatic Christian, supposedly skilled or learned in spiritual matters and experiences. I thought about it for a moment. I was dead inside, felt lost, and did not really have any hope for my future. I knew that I did not want to surrender and conform to a mindless, spiritless consumer lifestyle in the suburbs. Yet I did not know how to become more spiritual relatively safely — without destroying myself in the process.

"OK, I will see her. How soon can I meet her?" I replied. The necessary telephone calls were made.

I met Anna a week later in early August, 1977. She asked me

questions about my life while she shared parts of her life story with me. She was a German Jew who had escaped Nazi Germany as a young woman. She found her way to the United States. At some point she converted to Roman Catholicism. She then became baptized in the Holy Spirit of God. She had various gifts such as alleged tongue speaking; a very strong presence in prayer; certain sensitivities or spiritual discernment such that she often accurately knew what people were thinking and feeling or how the person might be struggling in their faith; and as the Spirit willed, the gift of healing by the laying on of hands. She did not bluntly declare these things to me. Rather, she either shared them with me during the first few sessions or I witnessed the gifts or qualities.

The thing that still stands out as initially very irritating about her was her pushy insistence that I become born-again the first time we met at her home in Long Grove. With her, it was the absolute prerequisite for a new, deeper spiritual life. If I was to have any hope or to grow far beyond where I was in my life and current state of being, I first had to become reborn in Jesus Christ.

Soon our time for that first meeting ended. I was going canoeing with my brother the next week, so Anna and I planned to meet again two weeks from that first meeting, near the end of August 1977. Again, as I was walking out of her house to my car, she stood in the doorway urging me to become reborn.

"Mark, you have to become reborn."

"OK. Thanks. I'll think about it while I'm canoeing. I will let you know when I get back," I said as I walked to my car.

She baked good bread and seemed nice, but she certainly seemed pushy.

The canoe trip was OK. My brother and I went to the upper St. Croix River on the border of Wisconsin and Minnesota. It is a very beautiful area. However, I was preoccupied with the curious set of circumstances that led me to Anna after hearing the voice in the movie theater lobby. I really wondered if I should try becoming reborn, if it would change things for the better.

Quite frankly, I didn't see why I had to become reborn. I had been praying to God on and off my entire life. Christ had helped me many, many times already, sometimes openly. He knew where I lived and I knew how to get in touch with Him. Why did I have to comply with the extra requirement of becoming reborn? What I knew of born-again Christians was that they seemed somewhat fanatical or hysterical, and not to be deep thinkers: teary eyed, simplistic, dogmatic rednecks for Jee-zuss; frequently with bad haircuts and boring clothing! Who needs that?

People in many churches tend to view born-again Christians with disdain or amusement. For them, praying to be "born-again" borders on the ridiculous. For hundreds of years many people have developed a deep love for and fidelity to God directly due to believing and practicing the Biblical teachings of their respective churches. That is one of the values of participating in a great spiritual tradition such as the Orthodox, Roman Catholic, Anglican, and Lutheran churches, among others.

Often it seems that those people who espouse the need to become born-again have simply created an extra requirement out of their need to distinguish their faith or to be different. They have rediscovered the wheel from a different perspective, that is all. Perhaps if their sect or denomination had the spiritual richness and depth contained in the traditions mentioned above, they would not need the hyperfocus on "becoming born-again".

Also, praying to be born-again does not distinguish most of those people as being more kind, loving, civil, patient, and so forth than people in the older Christian churches. People are who they are. Authentic transformation is a process, not the result of any one prayer. Praying to become born-again is not a magic phrase that instantly transforms a person into perfection or automatic growth Rather, it is a challenging lifetime practice of prayer and right action that, in hidden partnership with the Holy Spirit working in us, transforms us into powerful and charismatic reflections of Christ Jesus.

In summary, being reborn in the Holy Spirit is necessary to

follow Jesus and to receive the gift of eternal life, but there is more than one specific way or process for people to surrender in love with God. Love is always a process of mutual surrender and openness, not an instant intimacy. The process produces authenticity. All throughout the history of Christianity, there have been different ways and cultural styles for believers to enter into deeper relationship with God through Christ. The commonality, even with born-again churches, is that of surrender in the deepest part of a person's being, a deference of will to the Holy. This is beyond any emotion or religious feelings and beyond any intellectual assent, although the surrender of one's will to God subsumes both the intellect and the heart. To deepen in love and life is to be ever more open and ever more deeply surrendered to the Other Person.

Having said this, though, in some cases, it does appear best for a person to make a clean break from their past by praying to God asking for a new self, a new life hidden in Him. This was the case for me, I just did not know it yet.

One night while my brother and I were sitting around our campfire on an island in the middle of the river, we were visited by a very strong evil presence. We tried to ignore it, to shrug it off as just our imaginations, but the evil presence only grew more pronounced. As always, there was a crushing or oppressive feeling. We were struggling to control our fear. Had we been closer to where we parked my car and had there been more light, we might have left the area. We were stuck where we were, so we decided to get in the tent and hide in our sleeping bags, hoping the evil would go away. I probably prayed to God for protection. Fortunately, nothing more than a deep terror happened. The remainder of our canoe trip passed without incident. We returned safely home. Interestingly, spiritual evil often visits people who are about to make a deeper commitment to Christ. It tries to intimidate and frighten those people into not following through with the "marriage ceremony".

Later that week I returned to Anna's house to meet with her.

53

I told her of the evil presence on the canoe trip. Again, she talked about my need to become reborn by renouncing my current life and asking for a new one from God. I really felt that she was pestering me. As with the first session, I ended this one by promising to consider becoming reborn. When I arrived home, my mother was not there. I was alone.

"What the heck, I'll try it. If it doesn't work, I can always try some other path."

I went up to my room and gathered up all of my pipes, a scale, the marihuana, the hashish, some speed pills, and the copies of skin magazines that I had at the time. I took it all back downstairs, placing it on the hearth. I started a roaring fire in the fireplace. I then began tossing in all of the items I had just gathered from my room. As I did this, I prayed aloud asking for a new life in Christ, renouncing my old one. I renounced my old habits, apologizing to God.

From the moment that I prayed to be reborn in God's Spirit, I was instantly blessed with new life, real, indestructible hope, and a quiet, deep assurance or solidification of my being. The emptiness and hopelessness have never returned since that day approximately 25 years ago. True, there have been several periods, sometimes lasting several months, when I have been filled with pain or profound confusion, but since that day in August 1977 I have never been completely hope-less, empty, or lost. Rather, I have always known and trusted God and His Will for me. I have trusted that some way, somehow He would return to my awareness again. I have trusted that the pieces of my life would rotate and spin into new, greater, deeper, stronger life and meaning. He has never failed me in this. I am confident that He never will.

Another gift that I received during this period of spiritual regeneration is poetry. Before becoming reborn, I had written only one or two poems. Since my regeneration, I have written several dozen poems, some of which appear throughout this book. It is a special gift that only a Creator could give. By living open to or surrendered to the Holy Spirit, the many gifts are blossoming, finding fuller expression and use.

During my first month of new life in Christ, many expanded reality events occurred. As profound, confusing, or spectacular events had been before this time, those events pale in comparison to the dozens of events that have occurred and continue to occur since surrendering to Jesus Christ and His Holy Spirit. Trust me, I wasn't looking for any of these events to occur. The events simply happened, and continue to happen from time to time.

My decision to surrender my life back to God triggered an entire series of events as if I had pressed "Enter" on a computer keyboard. Instantly I changed. Certain psychic abilities were taken away or changed. Other gifts were given to me. New powers and processes became a part of my new being, and my default parameters were forever changed. It was a cosmic download and reconfiguration of my inner being. Long before there was the Internet, there was and is the mystical Body of Christ. I had just signed online.

Within a day or two of my metamorphosis, I began to feel hatred and anger directed at me. I recognized the source of those personal spiritual attacks. It was from the demonic forces who have chosen to war against God and all beings who choose to remain loyal to Him. One day while washing my hands, reality parted to the left of the sink as if a breeze gently blew away the mist of this world. I was suddenly gazing into the black void of the spiritual world (or at least the hallways between here and the next world). Off in the distance was a demon, unaware that I was staring at it. It must have felt me looking at it because it looked directly at me, then bolted out of view like a startled deer. I finished washing my hands, dried them, then exited the bathroom pondering what had just happened. I thought it was odd, but the demon was red and had horns and a tail, similar to certain classical portrayals of demons. The event was not a hallucination. I know what hallucinations are from drug usage. This event was real. Hallucinations lack certain components of reality. Any sane person can recognize the difference between a hallucination and reality, usually rather quickly.

Nor did I "wish" the vision, wanting to have a spiritual experience. It was a totally uninvited event and there was absolutely no need for the demon to appear in "classical" form aside from the simple conclusion that that must be what it looks like naturally. Even in 1977 I had enough experience with evil not to require it to appear in a cliché image so that I might recognize it.

I also began to have very vivid and disturbing dreams during the first few weeks after becoming reborn. Many of them were so real that I still question whether all of them were just dreams. I do think that at times I did astral project or naturally leave my body to travel to other "places" and to interact with other beings. It was strange. A month earlier the only things that were really bothering me were my emptiness and the Holy Spirit calling me to new life. Now, my emptiness was gone but suddenly I was under tremendous and frequent intense spiritual attack, both while awake and while sleeping.

Later that week (it was early September) I returned to Anna's house as scheduled. I shared with her all the events of the past week. She was pleased to hear that I had decided to become reborn. She placed her hands on my head and began praying. She prayed for God to baptize me with His Holy Spirit and for me to receive the gift of tongues. Most Pentecostal or Charismatic Christians believe that to be truly wedded to Christ a person must not only become reborn but must also be baptized in the Holy Spirit. This baptism is a separate event from becoming reborn.

Baptism in the Holy Spirit is believed to empower the believer with all sorts of gifts, abilities, and sensitivities that enable the believer to live more closely with God, sense other people's needs easier, and be empowered for greater holiness. However, it seems to me that I had already been baptized by God in His Holy Spirit years earlier, if being baptized in the Holy Spirit is a separate event from a full surrender to of heart, will, and mind to

Christ. Whether I became baptized when Anna placed her hands on my head and prayed is questionable. It is clear to me that God has always been with me in an undeniable and dramatic, tangible presence all of my life. I just have not always known it or appreciated it.

I specifically question whether I ever received the gift of tongues, specifically when Anna prayed for me. Honestly, I felt nothing when she prayed; no heat, no warmth, no power flowing into me even though she said I would experience all those feelings as the Spirit baptized me. Anna seemed a little disappointed when I reported the same to her. She prayed again, but I still noticed nothing extraordinary. She then said that I should simply pray in tongues by moving my tongue. I thought of a person running on a day with no wind trying to fly a kite. The person is vainly hoping that wind will catch it and carry it high into the sky. So I began moving my tongue, trying to mimic her. This was in sharp contrast to the foreign language I was naturally and fluently speaking during a demon fighting "dream" I had earlier that year, long before being born again or knowing what the gift of "tongues" was. To me, that 'combat patrol' with angels was more authentic because I was not trying to do anything at all; it just happened. I prayed the same language the angels prayed in. It was Latin or something, definitely not English.

Certainly, speaking in tongues is not conclusive proof that a person has been baptized in the Holy Spirit of God. Nevertheless, I spent the next 16 months "praying in tongues" thinking I was doing the right thing, that I had been blessed with that gift. There is a definite overemphasis on tongues throughout the Church today. I believe that the true gift of tongues is more rare than common, and is overrated compared to more important gifts such as a deep, honest, and open compassion (including tolerance) for people and the planet. Too much attention and importance are placed on it by too many people around the world, especially as the sign that a person has the Holy Spirit.

At the end of that first session with Anna after I became

reborn, she told me that I now had to make a life confession. It is a way of properly starting a new life, wiping the slate clean in a sense. I met with Fr. O'Leary the following week. After my confession, I went to the sanctuary to pray some more. It was at this time that Jesus walked up to me, telling me that He was "pleased with my decision." I was ecstatic and somewhat bewildered by His appearance. (See the next chapter, My Grain Of Sand). The next time I met with Anna, I told her of the vision. She took it in stride, seeming genuinely pleased for me.

On that day that I met with Anna, it was a beautiful autumn day. We decided to sit in the sun porch just off the back of her living room. While sitting there with our eyes closed in prayer, Jesus appeared to me again. As always, it was like watching a holographic movie. Seeing Him or any of the demons at other times was not a hallucination nor was it an image that arose from within me such as a dream or a thought. These events were separate and self-directed apart from my mind and consciousness. The vision of Jesus that He gave me on Anna's sun porch was symbolic compared to the previous ones.

He stood in front of me in a gleaming white robe, facing me. His arms extended downwards at His sides with the palms of His hands facing me. I forget which forearm He raised first but He raised one of them, bringing an image to His side. It was me. On His other side, He raised His other forearm and brought an image of my father to Him. Then my mother's image appeared and moved up to His side next to my father. Then my sister and brother slid over next to me. Our two dogs trotted by in front of all of us. We were arranged as if we were standing together for a group photograph. Jesus then swept His hand in front of the assemblage and small gleaming boxes appeared. I immediately understood these boxes to represent various blessings. Then He came forward, right up to my face.

"This I do for you,".

As before, He faded out as quickly as somebody "beaming up" on Star Trek or Voyager.

I excitedly told Anna about this when she finished praying. Again, her matter-of-fact acceptance was important and reassuring to me. Anna quickly understood that it was a symbolic vision from God promising to heal my deep wounds and to give me many blessings. Jesus had promised to heal me internally, not externally with my family members. On the other hand, I only believed that He was going to reunify my family physically and emotionally because that is what I wanted to believe. I did not appreciate or understand my need for deep healing. I misunderstood what He promised me, trying to change it to my understanding if I just believed it hard enough.

Even though there was violence and stress in my family, the legal separation my mother secured when I entered the hospital during the Christmas season of 1976 was very painful for all of us. I told my family about the vision. Not surprisingly, my parents were not thrilled with my interpretation of it, and were resistant to my imposed or desired interpretation. My brother and sister seemed happy about it but not quite certain how much credence the promise should have. Fortunately, by Spring 1978 I was beginning to question my forced belief that Jesus had promised to reunite my family. I was beginning to see and accept the deeper truth of inner healing versus the outward form I wanted.

I saw Jesus one more time during this initial period of new life in His Holy Spirit. My encounters and battles with demons in "dreams" and feeling their hateful dead energy arrows calmed down after a few weeks. Besides trying to intimidate me or confuse me, evil sought to entice me with lies of power and pleasure if I would just renounce Christ. I briefly contemplated those offers, before clearly rejecting them. My course was set.

Chapter 7
My Grain of Sand

Within two weeks of renouncing my old life and my old faith, I completed my fresh start by giving a life confession to Fr. O'Leary. After my confession, I walked back into the church sanctuary and knelt down in a pew to pray. Giving a confession and then trusting that my sins had been forgiven was a tremendous experience. Like throwing off a heavy, wet blanket, the weight of my first 19 years of life was lifted off my shoulders. I felt lighter, liberated and renewed or energized. I was the only one in the sanctuary. It was quiet and still, a cozy and peaceful darkness. I could hear an occasional miscellaneous sound or two from the direction of the church office, around the corner and down a short hallway. I closed my eyes in thoughtful conversation with and prayer to God.

A few moments later, while my eyes were still closed, Jesus Christ walked up to me. That is, He appeared approximately "30 feet" away (in space-time measurement judging by His size when He first appeared) from me to my left between me and where the altar is situated. As if walking in our world, He turned right onto the main aisle of the church sanctuary and proceeded directly to me.

I had seen Him once before when I needed His help a couple years earlier in October 1975. At that time, expecting nothing fantastic, I was awed to see Him appear in response to my prayers for help and peace. However, I did not get a clear look at Him then because He was farther away from me and He was radiantly clothed in pure, crystal, white light. He was a brilliant white sun.

This time was very different. I saw Him as real and as clearly as anyone sees anyone else in our world. Although my experience might be labeled "visionary", there was nothing ethereal or unreal about it. It was no different than channel surfing or using the picture-in-picture feature on your TV: click click and now you are tuned into a very different program. Even though the original program you were watching and the current program are distinctly separate, both are equally "real". Likewise, the probability of there being other worlds and other planes of existence is not lessened just because this one is real and is the only one we know or are most familiar with — just ask any cosmologist or theoretical physicist. Our world and the spiritual world are somehow interlinked or connected.

Jesus was at once both beautiful and severe. He exuded great power and authority that expressed as radiant luminosity. He was wearing a white robe with a ceremonial rope at the waist. His hair was down to the middle of His back. There was no trace of silly sentimentality or weakness in His demeanor or face. Rather, He had a commanding charisma, an absolute and persuasive peaceful confidence. He walked right up to me and spoke with a directness and clarity that remains unmatched to this day.

"I am well pleased with your decision. I have important works for you to do."

He then faded out. I opened my eyes to an empty church, the same as when I had entered it a few minutes earlier. I sat there for a few minutes in stupefied wonder, trying to figure out what He meant.

I learned very quickly that this encounter was best kept to myself. The best intentions of my friends and acquaintances could not penetrate the mystery of His statements to me. For others, it was too weird or jealousy interfered with their attempts at helping me understand my relationship to Christ and who I might be as defined by that primary relationship. The event did not fit within their constructs of who God is and how He should behave. Other times, I was too arrogant to accept other people's opinions or at least to listen to what they were trying to tell me. The interplay of all of these responses to my encounter with Christ Jesus prompted me to shut up about the event.

I have never been able to forget about it even though in times past, on occasion, I tried to. That vision created a strong tension in me that has often left me confused, forced to sit on the cold, hard, lonely bench of patience. I have tried to live my own life within its earthly context but I could never forget His presence nor His statements that He wants me to do something for Him. After this vision, it always seemed a little absurd applying for a various jobs such as selling office equipment or deciding which brand of paper towels to buy, knowing that there is this larger, profound reality lurking just beyond the edge of our collective consciousness that exerts a profound pull on us like the unseen moon moving ocean tides in and out.

Positively, this expectation of some type of service for Him has repeatedly inspired and encouraged me to do good works. I have often taken risks beyond what I might normally have taken in order to help others or re-mind people of God's presence and love for us. Usually simple, human things such as showing kindness to different people, looking directly into the eyes of homeless people and sharing a smile with them (whether or not I give them money), giving a stranger a place to sleep and eat for a day or two when they needed it, and so forth. His words to me have helped focus me on emulating Him in our world, trying to quietly make it a better place, transforming or denying darkness, anger, and selfishness.

However, no matter what I have done over the years, I have always felt that whatever good work I did was not what He really wanted me to do, that there was something more that I was supposed to do. I have been waiting over 24 years. Thankfully, writing this book has taken away some of the inner restlessness I have carried all these years.

Due to my tension, my unrest, my confused expectation of waiting upon the Lord, I have not been able to commit myself fully to anything else, at least not for long periods of time. This has been very frustrating for me. Just as frustrating and disappointing have been my attempts at finding a career path that truly called or "fit" me, something that I was suited for until I began writing. For over half my life, I have been in the world but not quite of it, whether I like it or not. I have been unable to get lost in this world. Restlessness from within and without has not allowed me to settle into a general contentment. Like a grain of sand in an oyster, it has never really ceased to irritate me: the waiting; the mystery; the not quite fitting in; the inability to forget God or for Him to forget me.

Because of this distress I have, in times past, rebelled against God, being angry or impatient with the process of waiting. Other times, I have taken sinful advantage of my belief that Jesus wanted me specifically to do something for Him by acting in a selfish manner, feeling and acting "bullet-proof" by engaging in foolish behavior. Mixed in with my expectation and impatience, I have also worked very hard with Christ to heal from the toxic legacy of my first 19 years of life in the hope and intent to live a better life.

However, no matter what, I have always returned to Him. I am irresistibly drawn back like a moth to a patio light or a salmon returning to it's stream of origin. God has given me a great thirst for Him. Like a patient, loving parent, He tolerated and forgave my prodigal wanderings while coaching and encouraging me to grow up, to become mature in Him. Although He has never been impatient with me, He has at times become tired of my repeating of an error or certain sin. He has warned me a few times regarding the imperative of obedience to His Holy Spirit and the dangers of persistent disobedience, of being stiff-necked.

From the context of various events and periods in my life He has taught me much about His infinite compassion for all people and His infinite capacity to forgive; His woundedness; His desires and hopes; His anger and judgment; His concerns for all of us. In a very real sense, I believe to understand from Him that it is not easy being Christ, just as it is not easy being a loving and involved parent. I really believe that Jesus Christ bleeds as much today for all of us as He did in the garden shortly before His trial and execution two thousand years ago in Jerusalem.

As much as I have been irritated or exasperated waiting on Him, I have in the past been afraid or fearful of what my life is to be. There are several reasons for these fears. It has been both the human fear of the unknown, as well as the anxiety of trusting that unseen Someone Else to guide and protect my life, to offer ultimate meaning for my existence. Other times it has been spiritual evil attacking me, planting fears in my mind. I believe this to be accurate because the moment I pray certain prayers rebuking evil, the fears and oppression immediately leave me or "lift off" me. I have also experienced the healthy anxiety of being responsible for my own decisions and living my life as fully and properly as I am able. Along the way over the past 24+ years, I have come to understand and accept the humbling realization that I really control very little in life except my own attitude, my own faith response. That is, my response-ability.

Like almost everyone else, I have at times felt profoundly lost. Although I have known for much of my life that this world is not my home and that I came from God, I walk with God, and I will return to God, I have been in some big deserts. I have felt very lost and lonely. At times, clouds of doubt have blown into my eyes, blurring my vision. Mirages of fears and temptations have danced around me as I stumbled forward. Other times I have experienced something more like the thickest, wettest fog imaginable, barely illuminated by a weak diffuse gray light, while drifting on an unseen current. But always and everywhere eventually I feel the omnidirectional signal or beacon of Christ's Presence and His call to me to be with Him. He is truly my rock in the flood, giving me a fixed point by which to navigate life.

CHOOSING SIDES

FIST GRIP vs. ROOTS GRIP

self —-

    uptight

        grip   grip   grip

           my way!

Brittle
    break

busted pain.

      I want it!
          Make it happen now!

    oops! It's gone...

      Soft love
        gently growing

          almost casually...

The roots ever more deeply
    binding quietly together.

Chapter 8

Hydroplaning

Our encounters with evil are usually a part of our everyday lives in the human realm: our private dysfunctions or struggles; other people; disease; death; bad weather; and so forth. It is a pervasive force or spirit that tends to flavor or color nearly everything we experience, whether in thought, word, or deed. However, in addition to usually experiencing evil as a generalized force or spirit, there are beings in the spiritual realm that seem to be as purely evil as most angels seem holy. In fact, many of us, from time to time and usually unsolicited, have experienced evil beings from the next world poking into ours. Commonly known as demons, there seem to be other created beings — angels gone bad — who are rebelling against the Center of Life. It truly seems that we are born into the middle of a great conflict that we did not start and that we cannot end, we can only choose sides.

The first period of my deeper spiritual development and friendship with God remains somewhat of a mystery to me. I hydroplaned spiritually for about a year just after surrendering my old life to Christ in August, 1977. Hydroplaning occurs when driving a car on wet pavement such that a thin film of water separates the car tires from the road without the driver knowing it. It is always disturbing to realize that you were not in full control even though you thought that you were or to admit to yourself that you had misplaced trust.

The following is what happened to me. I have since learned that I am not unique in my experience of an angelic or spirit guide. Many people, from Christians to New Agers, may be hydroplaning or in danger of doing so nowadays. Whether a person wears crystals or a crucifix, no one is immune from being deceived by beings somewhat superior to us, superior in that they are able to look in on us as well as see more of the larger universe in comparison to our linear, earthbound awareness.

Shortly after becoming reborn in Christ, I began to hear a whispering voice "in" my head. I heard this voice on and off from September 1977 until early January 1979. I did not ask for it. I did not look for it. It just began occurring. I had already heard God speak to me through a variety of methods, including an audible voice, so hearing a spiritual voice on a regular basis did not seem totally unbelievable or implausible to me. Because my Christian spiritual teacher, Anna, and I had prayed for the "cleansing" of my "spiritual bloodlines"; and I had given a life confession; and Christ had walked up to me and spoke to me; I did not really suspect that I could also have a spirit guide that was not from God, but I had one. The spirit alternately claimed to be either Jesus or an angel as it guided me.

I tested the spirit or at least thought that I did many times when I had it with me, especially during the first couple months after it first befriended me. I asked the spirit who it was and if Jesus Christ incarnated into our world. St. John wrote that we should test the spirits we may encounter to see if they confess that Jesus Christ incarnated into our world. Supposedly every spirit that does is of God, while every spirit that does not is in rebellion against God. I thought I tested the spirit but in retrospect I have always wondered if I was really answering myself so I could continue hearing it. I do not definitely know. Importantly, foolishly, I thought that I was above being deceived. In fairness to myself, over 1900 years have passed since John wrote about testing the spirits in the manner just mentioned. Perhaps because following Jesus Christ has grown into a global religion, deceiving spirits now admit that God incarnated as a human. Perhaps a new test needs to be devised, if possible and useful.

What made the situation even more confusing was that mixed in with the guidance of the whispering spirit guide, I have no doubt that I was also often hearing or feeling the voice of the Holy Spirit or Jesus during that time. God certainly did not aban-

70

don me. However, I was an arrogant and ignorant young Christian who was unable as well as unwilling at times to recognize regularly and clearly true guidance from God versus guidance from other spirits or my own wishful thinking. I think that what probably happened is that Jesus allowed a demonic spirit to function as a special guide to train and test my faith and for me to develop skill in spiritual discernment as well as perhaps using me as an example or warning for other people.

It was very flattering to suddenly have a spirit guide. It fueled my need, my hope, my belief that I was "special" or that I had a special mission in the world. Sadly, I helped deceive myself, ignoring my own gut feelings or confusion many times in order to not have the spirit be wrong. I didn't trust myself and what I knew should be correct. I often and willingly assumed that somehow I was wrong or did not hear the voice correctly just so I could continue hearing it. Had I been honest with myself, not discounting my doubts and knowledge of things that I really knew to be incorrect, I would not have wasted the first several months of my new life following the deceiving spirit.

In retrospect, I recall that whenever God spoke with me, His Spirit's voice was always more clear, more direct, more certain in such a way that I really knew it was Him. When He speaks, His words possess you and resonate through you easily and deeply like a subsonic tremor that you feel more than hear. Although you might try to deny what you just heard, it remains and cannot be entirely disregarded. Put another way, unlike various spirits that communicate with humanity, He speaks with eminent domain. This remains true through today, although I usually no longer hear Him speaking to me with words directly within my consciousness. Being God, He can speak with anyone anywhere anytime in whatever way He chooses. He has wavelengths for communicating with His universe of created worlds that are beyond any bandwidth of created consciousness.

In contrast, because the spirit is a created being as I am, it's voice was often faint, similar to a radio signal on a stormy night:

not always clear reception. Also, it was frequently coy. The deceiving spirit acted innocent or evasive whenever events in this world did not unfold as it had told me they would. There were many times when it was immediately apparent that the spirit was wrong. Those times angered me. Yet in my need to believe in the spirit as being a special guide sent to help me — because I was "special" — as well as my fearful hesitation to demand that it leave me for fear of offending or losing God (a fear of abandonment which many others share), I bent over backwards to explain away whatever errors (lies) occurred. Although I correctly and naturally felt that the spirit was playing with me, and that it really wasn't God or God's spokesman to me, I was weak in a sense and instead found fault with myself instead of with the demon spirit. I wanted to continue to trust the voice because the extra knowledge it shared with me was an impressive and seductive comfort in the face of the apparent existential randomness of life.

Often during those first 12 - 16 months of new life in Christ, the spirit provided impressive guidance, as distinct from accurate or holy guidance. I was very impressed with the sudden ability I had to know when I should speak to different people about various spiritual or Christian concerns. I also knew ahead of time that certain events in daily life would occur. I did not need precognition, which was removed from me when I became born again. I had my spirit guide to provide knowledge of near-future events, telling me that it was from God to help me and others.

Curiously, I never detected the presence of evil in the spirit, although I wondered many times. However, I often did not have inner peace during that first year of new life in Christ, either. But I was too ignorant and stubborn to clearly discern between the Holy Spirit and the deceiving spirit guide. I know I tested the Holy Spirit's patience often during those first several months.

The spirit provided me with a mix of truth and lies, which is the definition of heresy. It encouraged my efforts to cram myself into Christianity, to be perfect immediately instead of through a maturation process filled with and guided by grace from God. The spirit urged and pushed me to try, try, try to be as perfect as possible by encouraging me to pray or to read scripture or whatever. The effect created a spiritual strait-jacket. The spirit guide was guiding me toward spiritual burnout. Sadly, I thought I was really on the road to holiness and was pleasing God through a rigorousness that lacked balance and grace. It provoked me to rebel and ignore God because I needed "down time" from the hard work of the manufactured holiness.

The spirit also manipulated my deep desire or need to serve God in order to subtly mislead me, separating me from God without my becoming alarmed. Part of the strategy was to lead me into good acts and to tell me things that were true. These experiences made it easier for me to tell myself that the spirit had my best interests in mind. I was able to share my new faith with several people during that first year, many met through the guidance and direction of the spirit.

An example is when it instructed me to wait by a certain table in the student union at a local junior college. The spirit specifically told me to wait for a certain older woman, who was a complete stranger, to walk by. I was then to speak to her, saying whatever the spirit suggested or instructed me to tell her. Because I said things unknown to me that touched the stranger deep inside, she stopped and we began talking. In this context I was able to talk with her about Jesus. It turns out that she had many questions regarding Christianity and quickly agreed to meet with me again to continue talking. Without the deceiving spirit guiding me, I would have never met her. As amazed as she may have been about our meeting because she had been praying for guidance or teaching, I was even more impressed.

Another example of the spirit telling me "inside" information occurred when I was at an acquaintance's house for Thanksgiving Dinner 1978. By this time I had basically stopped believing that the spirit was Jesus or a friendly angel. Yet I still did not quite have the courage to rebuke it with any finality. As well, it was persistent, exploiting my taciturn resolve to firmly reject it. For me, it was like an irritating person with whom I had once been friends, of whom I could ask questions of whenever I wanted answers, or to get an extra awareness of events in life.

I was watching a football game with one of the other guests. He was only about 12 years old at the time. He had a reputation of being 100% accurate in picking the winners and losers, often by the exact point spread. This was very impressive. The adults at the dinner were in awe of his uncommon ability. All of this caused me to wonder if he had a spirit guiding him. I prayed, asking "Jesus". The voice told me that he was in fact possessed. I did not say anything to anybody but I did silently pray for him and his freedom.

A few years later my father gave me an unsolicited update on the boy. He told me that when the boy went to receive his first communion, he became violently angry and was cursing and speaking in Latin or some other language. A couple of people had to restrain him. Shortly thereafter he underwent the Rite of Exorcism conducted by Roman Catholic priests. If any of this is accurate or true (and I have no reason to doubt it because my father did not follow Christ), it is another example of how my spirit guide had superior knowledge and insight compared to me and most other people.

Interestingly, years later I happened to read chapter 16 in the Book of Acts in the New Testament of the Bible. There is a brief story, written approximately 1940 years ago, of a slave girl whose owners made their living off of her ability to predict future events. For several days the spirit in her harassed Paul and the others with him in the city of Philippi (in modern day Greece) every time they walked past the place where the slave girl hung out. Finally one day, in exasperation, Paul rebuked the evil spirit and commanded it to leave the girl in the name of Jesus Christ. The spirit left immediately, causing the slave girl to lose her psychic abilities. Consequently, because her owners lost their means of making easy money, they sued Paul in the local court system.

It's funny how the more things change, the more they stay the same.

A third example of how the spirit provided guidance to me is when I asked it where UFOs come from after seeing the movie "Close Encounters of the Third Kind" in Spring 1978. The spirit told me that UFOs are manifestations that come from the spiritual world to deceive humanity for some reason(s) or agenda it did not explain to me. I had not thought of that possibility until I asked the spirit. If what the spirit said is true, then we should all be very concerned. Whether or not it is really true remains to be proven. It is interesting, however, that people who claim to have been abducted by aliens usually describe horrible rapes of their bodies and minds. Makes you wonder.

During the months that I earnestly believed or wanted to believe that the spirit was Jesus or an angel from God, I basically removed myself from accountability to other serious Christians who were more mature and more experienced. There were two reasons. First, I did not really want to lose the "privilege" of having the spirit guide. Second, most people have never experienced a spirit guide or even many expanded reality events thus making their counsel usually insufficient or very limited due to their lack of experience with such matters. I did not need to hear any more simplistic or heartfelt advice or knee jerk reactions.

However, there were times when the spirit's true nature should have been clearly obvious to me. Yet due to my enjoyment of the power of the special knowledge, I willingly helped deceive myself, inadvertently impeding God's deepening presence in my life. I did not recognize and get alarmed by the problems or sin that the spirit openly and tacitly promoted in me for the "down times" when I needed to rest and rebel from the hard work of instant holiness, from cramming myself into Christianity. By most accounts, I was living a very holy and consecrated life during my first twelve months of new life in Christ. Yet one day, while driving down Rte 14 from Barrington to

Palatine, Illinois, I complained to Jesus about how much I had given up for Him and how I no longer had any fun. I complained about having given up sex and marihuana to follow Him. At that moment I sensed the spirit speaking to me under the pretense of being Jesus. It told me that smoking pot again would be OK. I double checked, but it reassured me that it was OK to smoke pot because I was so holy and advanced in other ways that the sin of drugs would be temporarily tolerated by God. Per the spirit, smoking pot was my "safety valve" for all of the effort and hard work I was doing to become instantly perfect in Christ. Clearly, I did not know or trust that Jesus is lovingly patient and powerful in guiding the process of our transformation into the people of God. I was unintentionally denying His power through rigorous godliness.

Sadly, I was too ignorant and stubborn to realize that I was forcing my opinion on God with the encouragement of the deceiving voice. The Holy Spirit was upset with my stubborn and rebellious behavior, kicking and bucking inside me like a wild horse. If I were more honest with the situation and myself, I would have known immediately that Jesus would never allow me or any other follower to continue smoking marihuana or to take any other drugs while trying to follow Him. Long after I shed the spiritual leach, I still used pot or some other drug on occasion due to lack of discipline and rebellion against God's gentle hand on my shoulders. This initial reopening of a door that should have stayed shut nearly shipwrecked my faith a couple of times.

The crowning lie from the spirit, the one that finally gave me the courage and the anger necessary to rebuke it decisively and to repent to God was when the spirit began telling me that I was a great prophet. After months of telling me this in various ways, either I asked or the spirit just gave me a dozen or so predictions to announce to others. The predictions would prove or confirm, for me and for others, my election as a prophet once the predictions came to pass. At the time I knew very little about Biblical prophecy. Like most people, I confused predictions such as what any common psychic can get and give with true prophecy from God. In general, God's prophetic communications are given by God through certain people whom He has chosen and prepared with the intent of moving people to repentance of personal or corporate sins, greater holiness, or the reassurance of His presence and involvement in our planetary history. My little spirit guide, not being of God, could only tell me predictions, not prophecies.

However, as mentioned above, I did not know the difference at the time. The one thing I did know was that if it was a prophecy from God, every word must come true within the explicit or implicit time frame for such occurrences if the alleged prophecy involved specific time frames. If the prophecy did not come to pass as announced, then the person who gave it was not speaking as a prophet of God. Every prediction came to pass within the time frames the spirit had given me except for the West Coast earthquake. The spirit told me it would happen by December 31, 1978. Thank God it actually happened twelve hours past the deadline on New Years Day 1979 between 12P - 2P Central Standard Time. I was relieved, very relieved.

I never really believed that I was some great prophet, it never "fit", it was too much cognitive dissonance, too much pressure. Also, I was very tired of the micro-management and religious rigorousness that the spirit had imposed on me. The true, living God is not and never has been and has no intention of being a micro-manager of human beings. He is a micro-sustainer in that we and all things exist only within and by the love of the Great Spirit, but He is definitely not a micro-manager. We are the micro-managers due to our needs for control, power, and domination over ourselves, others, and the environment.

I was tired of the idiosyncrasies and discrepancies between what the spirit would tell me and objective reality. Because the earthquake did not occur as predicted, I must not be a prophet. If I was not a prophet, then the spirit guide was not from God because it had really told me a lie (in addition to all the other lies

77

it had told me over the previous 16 months). Finally, I could firmly and confidently rebuke the spirit to leave me forever. Prior to this liberating failure, I was afraid to rebuke the spirit guide because I was worried that I might lose God if I did so.

The spirit tried, I believe, to return to me in the Autumn of 1979 during my first term at Oregon State University. However, I resisted it, told it to go away, and I drew even closer to God like a child hugging his mother's leg when a stranger is nearby. The spirit left me and has not been back since that time. Yet like bad friends from the old neighborhood that a person outgrows, I know that I could probably "go back" and renew the relationship with it. Fool me once, shame on you. Fool me twice, shame on me.

I asked God then and now when writing this book how I could have picked up the spiritual leach and then kept it for so many months. I believe that when I responded to the invitation of new life in August 1977, because evil could not intimidate me, or persuade me, it went to Plan 3: mislead and deceive me. It played on my then low self-esteem and my complementary over-correcting need to be somebody, to be important. Also, my desire to serve God was exploited. At the time, I loved God, but I was very new to a deeper, sustained relationship with Him. I did not clearly understand or recognize the Holy Spirit's gentle and frequently subtle guidance. I was also ignorant of the wisdom in the Bible that deals with spiritual deception. Had Jesus not appeared to me previously so that I knew He truly is alive and involved with our world, I am fairly certain that my faith would have died in January 1979.

I was relieved to be rid of the spirit who had been my "friend" but I was also devastated, angry, and confused. I felt stupid because I had let myself be duped and I was angry and confused about God, wondering why He let the situation happen, instead of protecting me. It is always upsetting and unsettling when your understanding of God either dies or fails due to something unexpected and painful hurting you or a loved one in some way. Most parents protect their children from harm rather than let their child experience harm, then warn them.

Fortunately, because I knew Jesus really existed, I reasoned simply that I had hydroplaned. I concluded I would have to achieve union and intimacy with God through a different type of relationship, details to be worked out as I went along. I immediately quit trying to cram myself into Christianity and holiness, opting instead for true existential authenticity. I stopped trying to be my idea of perfect. I gave God the freedom to take me as I was, trusting that my Creator would understand and would remain with me during His process of transforming me into a holy follower. I had to trust God more.

I realized that I had to trustingly, patiently accept the frightful tension between seeing how God sees me in truth, but that He loves and accepts me as I am; balanced with the dynamic stress of sensing from Him the person He calls and invites me to be. And He never shows more than a few meters in front of your life in the present – He doesn't permit you to out-drive the light of His friendship to try to see around the next corner. It is a very human impulse to try to avoid or dodge this vivid awareness, this creative tension.

If I was no longer in a hurry to be perfect, I certainly didn't need a spirit guide assisting me to accelerate my growth. To use an analogy, although it took about 16 months, I finally realized and trusted my coach that in order to become a spiritual athlete with a hard body, it would require the proper diet of sound teaching and doctrine, the serious exercise of personal discipline and daily prayer, and the proper rest of patience and quiet contemplation rather than using the steroids of spirit guides.

Another disturbing conclusion that I gleaned from the spirit guide experience is that there are intelligences or beings that exist in the next, contiguous reality whose sole purpose in life seems to be to mess with our hearts and minds. Anything they can do to prevent or disrupt our relationship with God is a victory for them. I remain deeply impressed by the depth of hatred many spirits seem to have toward us humans. It is similar to experiencing the hatred of other racial groups when you personally have never done anything against that racial group. I now understand and accept the fact that humanity lives in the middle of a great transreality conflict between beings loyal to God and those in rebellion. If evil, which at it's root is spiritual, cognizant, and self-willed, is so preoccupied or fixated on misleading and even destroying us humans, then it seems to be risky business for people to have spirit guides.

Likewise, many people today are giving inordinate and undiscriminating attention and praise or devotion (another word for worship) to angels. We really do not know fully what we are dealing with. Although most of us experience holy angels, perhaps as guardian angels, there are evil (non-holy, opposed to the Most High) angels, commonly known as demons. Because these beings exist independently of humanity, our belief, unbelief, or indifference about them does not change their existence. Ignoring gravity doesn't make it go away; the same is true of beings from other realms.

Like students in a classroom that has a two-way mirror in the back of the room, beings from outside our "classroom" can observe us and even interact with us, perhaps by entering our room, other times just tapping on the glass mirror to get our attention. However, we honestly have no idea who those beings are behind the "glass" and what their motives are regarding us because now 'we see through a glass darkly'. It is wise to remember what we tell our children: "stranger — danger".

Interestingly, I have heard people who are or have been witches speaking on various talk shows and in person about spirit guides that they have experienced or known. The similarities between their experiences and mine are striking. Also, many Christians who are "charismatic", those who believe that they have received certain (additional) spiritual gifts from the Holy Spirit, frequently hear voices that in retrospect misled them in various ways. As upsetting and shameful as my experience was, it seems the phenomenon is more common than the general public is aware of.

Test the spirits and take a close look at those people who claim to be in contact with God or with higher powers. Evaluate them and what they say and do in light of the revelation of Jesus Christ and of historical orthodox Christianity. As a starting point, a timeless resource are the letters and correspondence preserved in the New Testament of the Bible. "Do not let anyone who delights in false humility and the worship of angels disqualify you for the prize [which is eternal life through and union with Jesus Christ]. Such a person goes into great detail about what [s]he has seen, and his [her] unspiritual mind puffs him [her] up with idle notions." Colossians 2:18.

Unlike Christianity, which was directly inspired by a real flesh and blood person who died then rose from the dead and ascended into heaven, many other religions have been created or inspired by whispering voices or angels or spirit guides communicating to certain selected people at various times and places. In some cases, the alleged same angel inspired different religions that contradict each other. This begs the question of what is the real truth. Curiously, there are usually two commons elements shared by all non-Christian, angel-inspired religions. The first is a redefinition of Jesus from God-Man who was raised from the dead to something less profound and less anomalistic such as 'prophet' or 'elevated teacher'. The second follows from the first by promulgating a redefinition of how to receive the gift of eternal life other than through Christ.

"The Spirit clearly says that in later times some will abandon the faith and follow deceiving spirits and things taught by demons. Such teachings come through hypocritical liars, whose consciences have been seared as with a hot iron." 1 Timothy 4:1-2. "Dear friends, do not believe every spirit, but test the spirits to see whether they are from God, because many false prophets have gone out into the world.....You, dear children, are from God and have overcome them, because the one who is in you is greater than the one who is in the world. They are from the world and therefore speak from the viewpoint of the world, and the world listens to them. We are from God, and whoever knows God listens to us; but whoever is not from God does not listen to us. This is how we recognize the Spirit of truth and the spirit of falsehood." 1 John 4:1, 4-6. Although these strong words were written in letters nearly 2,000 years ago to the early Christian Church, they seem to be just as relevant today. We all must be careful. No one is immune to spiritual deception.

Chapter 9
Regroup

In January 1979 I was sorting things out while beginning my second semester at Trinity College in Deerfield, Illinois. I was glad I could just be myself again, whoever I was. I was tired, even exhausted. It is hard work trying to be religious, holy, and perfect when you are pushing for the perfection instead of the Holy Spirit leading and guiding you according to His timetable. I prayed a lot as I regrouped and assessed my experience. I prayed for insight, guidance, balance, and wisdom. I decided that God is the one who can truly transform and change people.

I cannot change the basic elements that make me who I am, my default parameters. Only God can do that because He is my Creator. What I can and should do is to pray for that change, granting permission to my Creator to change me as He deems necessary or desirable. God never violates our most primary and final boundary, our free will. He always leaves the final choice up to you and me, whatever that choice may be depending upon various circumstances. God has infinite respect for us — certainly more that we have for ourselves and for each other. Our role is to invite Him into our hearts, minds, and lives. Then we are to follow His lead or urgings for growth, service, and enjoyment; in short, a new life of meaning and pleasure. As we surrender to this gentle Holy Will, we become more ourselves and certainly more at peace and joy-full just as a guitar string vibrates to harmonies as it yields to tuning by a skilled musician.

I realized that God actually prefers an honest sinner to a follower who is so busy recreating their self that God ends up being in the way. You cannot rush the baking of bread, especially if you are the loaf being baked. An honest sinner is in a better position to hear the still voice of God and to feel the urgings of His Holy Spirit. God is a God of process more than instantaneous changes.

Thus, authentic healing, growth, and perfection of a human spirit or life are processes, at least in this world. I don't have to be perfect, just responsive.

The other significant conclusion I made during this time was really more of a revelation. It had to do with the manner in which I wanted God to interact and communicate with me. I told God that I did not want to hear any more voices. I did not want to be guided like that by His Holy Spirit. I also decided that I should not seek out a voice, that I should resist listening to any voices. We needed to relate and share with each other in a different manner. I courageously stated to God, myself, and "anybody else" who might have been listening that if God is truly God, then His Holy Spirit can guide me without me having to be consciously involved in the guidance. The Spirit can and will guide me intrinsically, intuitively. He doesn't need to use a mode of communication as unsophisticated and prone to error as a voice that I often had trouble hearing clearly anyway. God has channels of communication available to Him for speaking to His creation that no one or nothing else can interfere with.

In the years since, I have never really had serious difficulty knowing what, when, or where God is sharing with me. The exceptions have been one or two periods in my life that have long since passed. The only other times that I have had trouble hearing God speaking to my heart have been those times when I consciously chose to try to ignore Him for various lengths of time. Fortunately, more often than not, I have obeyed His gentle daily guidance, surrendering ever more deeply in loving trust to Him, which has allowed God to surrender more deeply in love to me.

God truly enjoys being with us and it offends or hurts Him when we do not let Him do so. It is similar to our children telling us to go away and not knock at their bedroom door when we really wanted to go in and spend time with them. It stings even though we might understand why our child told us to go away (i.e. wanting time to themselves). Wisely, I have become respectful and obedient to the heart whispers of the Holy Spirit. Over the years, I have been greatly blessed by the resultant relationship with God. An example, besides my survival of my first 19 years of life, is that how to live with the Holy Spirit helped prepare me for a relationship with my wife. I developed the habit of sharing my life, my time, my thoughts, and my feelings with God. I have learned to be available and attentive to God, His desires, needs, and requests. Both of these habits or skills have helped prepare me for daily intimacy with my wife. I learned that real relationships, especially healthy, intimate, loving relationships, are not instant or forced. Rather, they unfold and develop over time, becoming evermore graceful and nourishing.

Chapter 10

The Bridge in the Moonlight

Leaves had begun to fall in anticipation of an early Autumn in September 1983. A full harvest moon was in the sky at night. I was in the Cleveland, Ohio area visiting family and friends on a long weekend. Saturday night my friend, Alex, and I went out in search of fun and games. At the time, he lived about 25-30 miles south, southeast of downtown Cleveland, just on the edge of the metro area. Had we known what the evening had planned for us, we probably would not have left his house.

The first bar that we went to that night turned out to be the only bar that we went to. After just a couple of beers, we lost interest in being there. We were restless. We decided to move on.

"Well, what do you want to do?" I asked Alex. "What can we do that is interesting?"

"I don't know. You're my guest, so you decide."

Alex gave me the same answer every time I asked him what we could do that would be fun. It was getting aggravating.

For the next half hour we cruised around trying to decide what to do next to entertain ourselves. Alex felt that it was a good time to smoke some pot. His need for privacy while he lit up took us off the busier main roads and put us on hilly, semi-rural secondary roads.

Traveling in the pickup cab while he smoked made me tense. I didn't have the heart for fellowship with God that night. I wanted to pull back out of the light for awhile, to take a break and just be a human focused or absorbed in the details of our world, without having to think of Him. Although I knew that smoking pot was not good for me spiritually or physically, I also thought that it could create some distance from God for awhile. Even though at that point in my spiritual growth I was able to easily resist temptation such as pot *if I wanted to*, I had drank enough beer that night to more easily deny the Holy Presence in me. It is a sad but true basic urge of every human being to avoid the presence of God in varying degrees and frequency.

After a few minutes, I asked to take a couple puffs. Unlike Bill Clinton, I did inhale. I had just enough to put an extra spin on the beer buzz I already had. The moment I took the puffs, I felt regret and guilt for my sin. I immediately felt God's presence pull back from me both within and without. Or perhaps it was me pulling back from Him.

I knew from past sin that it would be several hours, perhaps longer, before the Spirit would return more fully to me again. The Creator of the Universe, Who mysteriously is a Person rather than a faceless Force, expects respect from His creatures. My being, one of His temples or vessels, needed cleansing for it had been defiled. Out of shame and a sense of failure, I did not want to think of Him. But He did not abandon me, He would not leave me alone.

Within a span of just 10-15 minutes God made His presence known to me in three different and startling ways that simultaneously prompted me to repent while assuring me that no matter what happens, He will always be with me.

We drove suddenly past one of those red and white roadside signs with a scripture quote on it. It appeared out of nowhere on one of the dark and lonely country roads that we were traveling on. Usually those signs are alongside busier roads. Because of my circumstances, it was surprising to see and read the sign. The quote urged repentance and belief in Jesus. As unexpectedly as it appeared, it disappeared back into the dark, outside the arc of the pickup truck headlights as we continued driving.

In an effort to feel a little more at ease, I began to adjust the truck radio looking for a good song to change my mood, to divert my mind. I paused for just a moment on a station, thinking that a song would be coming on. Instead, it was a Christian radio station. I turned the radio dial as soon as I realized that it was not a music station, but again, I felt God making eye contact with me or figuratively pushing on my chest with one of his fingers. I did not feel condemned but I knew that He knew that I knew I was wrong for getting high and rejecting His Presence. This revelation made me sad. I felt unworthy of his friendship and presence yet He would not leave me alone nor condemn me for what I did.

The strangest and most powerful assurance was God's last sign to me. Alex and I came to a four-way stop in the middle of nowhere. There were no houses or cars in the area. A lone light on a phone pole lit the intersection. As Alex made a perfunctory stop, I glanced around. On the far corner of the intersection was a school. The entire school and its grounds were dark except for one small light in a classroom. The light was a portrait or picture light attached to a picture frame. The light illuminated a lone portrait of Jesus Christ. Seeing it jolted me.

God had focused my attention back on Him in a way that I dared not try to ignore any longer. It was gentle but deeply disturbing. I could not hide from Him. I had wanted to have some time for just myself and my own will — as selfish as yelling at somebody for no other reason than to push them into leaving you alone for awhile. Smoking pot seemed like the way to offend Him enough to keep Him away for a couple of hours. Yet He was calling me back immediately, not forcefully or shamefully, but with the simplicity and clarity of forgiveness and understanding. I thought that my attitude and actions warranted greater censure or punishment, especially by my Creator. He was killing me with kindness. He wasn't trying to manipulate me or make me feel guilty, it is just that He is Love. He wasn't shaming or condemning me although I felt shame and regret regarding my behavior. I was painfully aware of my sin, my falling short of who I was able to be like a sharp shadow in the noonday sun. This awareness prompted me to repent and apologize. My buzz was gone, but I did not want it anymore.

As I prayed for His forgiveness and to feel His presence and touch again (similar to Psalm 51), I knew that no matter what happens in my life or what I do, I will never be "lost" or permanently separated from His love, His concern, His watchful gaze. That is, I may unilaterally lose awareness and feeling of His presence due to my actions or lapse in prayerful awareness but He will never forget or abandon me. As St. Paul wrote in the Book of Romans, I knew at that moment sitting in that pickup truck cab that "neither death nor life, neither angels nor demons, neither the present nor the future, nor any powers, neither height nor depth, nor anything else in all creation, will be able to separate [me] from the love of God that is in Christ Jesus our Lord." Romans 8:38-39. A few minutes later, this realization would be the difference between disaster and courage. Alex had no idea of my private conflict, nor my conversation with the Source Being of all things. I was carrying on two different conversations at the same time. It was like looking through the people and scene reflected in a restaurant window at night to the larger reality outside, beyond, and behind it.

"What do you want to do?" Alex asked again.

Just as I was ready to call it a night and suggest that we go back to his house to watch TV or even sleep, I remembered the old train bridge. I was not certain that he would say "Yes" to visiting it. I tossed the idea out to get his reaction.

"Hey, what about going to the old train bridge you showed me last May? It should be beautiful there tonight."

The steel bridge was one of his new "favorite places" that he had begun frequenting during the past year. He had taken me there the prior Spring on a beautiful day. The air was warm and fresh, gently scented with a thousand million plants and wildflowers celebrating a new growing season. Insects and birds flitted about. It was exhilarating to stand on the bridge and watch the river flowing quiet and swift through the spaces in the railroad ties. The river separates fields and flood plain to the west from a small forest along the narrower eastern side of the valley floor. The bridge is part of an abandoned track spur that runs west to east, ending at a shuttered mill a half mile south of the bridge. The valley sits at the southeastern end of the extensive Metro Park System that graces Cleveland like a wreath.

"OK. Good idea," Alex said without hesitating to think about it.

Both he and I enjoy being outdoors, even at night. He began pointing the truck down the two or three roads that we needed to travel to get to the truck trail that led to the bridge.

It was a perfect Autumn night to be outside, especially in the countryside. The night was clear with a full moon, the air as crisp as a fresh apple, and the landscape beautiful and mysterious, painted by the moon's soft, metallic light. Things normally known by sunlight were transformed into new and beautiful shapes, shadows, and textures. Adding to this alluring landscape was the layered mist or fog that frequently occurs in Autumn due to warm days and cool evenings. Sounds are transformed by the magic of the alternative light and the layers of gentle moonlit mist, sounding softer and slightly alien or surreal. We reached the turnoff within five minutes of my brilliant, evening-saving suggestion.

Much to my confusion, the moment Alex guided his pickup truck onto the winding dirt track I began to feel unrest and a feeling that I, we, should not be doing what we were doing. I didn't understand why. I couldn't think of any reason why I was suddenly feeling apprehensive. I quickly checked with a prayer and concluded that it was not God giving me the feeling as disapproval for doing something sinful. I was not doing anything "wrong" at that point. We had just reconciled. He does not grant His peace and awareness of His presence one moment only to revoke it the next to punish or manipulate people. He doesn't play games like that. There were no other reasons why I should feel guilty or anything, either. We weren't breaking any laws to drive back to the bridge. I was irritated with myself for having the feeling, worried that I was turning prematurely straight, becoming incapable of having spontaneous fun and adventure. I simply couldn't understand why alarm and now fear were welling up within me. Again, I did not share with Alex what was going on within me. I resolved to control my feelings, ignoring them if necessary. Alex parked in the same spot that we parked in the previous May.

As before, it was just a few steps from where we parked to get up on the raised, abandoned train bed. In the silvery blue moonlight, the bridge was easily visible 75 yards ahead. The dark forest lurked silently at the other end of the bridge. I was now very tense, still not knowing why. Alex and I were each carrying a bottle of beer to drink out on the bridge. The area was silent and the night was still beautiful. As far as we knew, no one else was within a couple miles of the bridge. A few clouds had drifted into the sky adding luminescent sculptures to the stars and moon.

Alex and I walked onto the bridge, stopped halfway across, and stood there for a couple minutes, drinking in all of our surroundings. I still didn't know why, but I could no longer ignore my fear. The area was supposed to be special, quite beautiful. Yet, like the first time Alex took me to the bridge, the area felt like a flat-spot in the rhythm of life. A dead stillness pervaded the scene.

Alex felt it too. Unlike our visit during the day in the Spring, he was not pushing me to climb up on top of the bridge trestle to sit. He just stood there, looking around. We both stood there confused and desireless like deer blinking in truck headlights, wondering why we were no longer enthusiastic about being on the bridge.

Like a rider struggling to control his spooked horse, I was suddenly fighting to control and suppress a powerful urge to run as fast as I could from the place. In talking with Alex later, he was struggling too. Neither one of us wanted to disappoint the other by suggesting that we leave the area. Nor, I suppose did we want to admit feeling uneasy being there on the bridge. Perhaps we were just trying to be macho. At least that is what was shooting through my mind as I struggled to control myself. The silence and stillness of the area now seemed menacing and weird. It heightened our growing, inexplicable terror.

CLINK.

A clear, distinct, metallic clink issued from the woods. Something or someone had to have made the noise that sounded like a heavy metal chain being handled, but we didn't see anybody or anything moving around the clearing just inside the woods, less than 120 feet away from where we were standing on the bridge.

"Did you hear that?" Alex asked.

"Hear what?" I replied knowing exactly what he was asking about, but refusing to acknowledge that something weird was happening.

"That noise, that clink."

"Oh, that was just my beer bottle hitting my belt buckle," I lied. I nervously tapped the glass bottle against my belt buckle hoping to reproduce the sound we had just heard from nowhere and no one in the woods.

I knew that I couldn't reproduce the sound but I was fighting to control the terror we both felt. We both wanted to believe my transparent lie because the truth that we were becoming aware of was too frightening to admit. I had conflicting impulses of standing glued in placed or running like (from) hell to get out of there. It was getting harder to think as terror constricted around our minds, squeezing tighter and tighter.

"Do you want to climb up on top (of the bridge trestle)?" Alex asked, just as he had in May during the daylight.

"No," I replied as calmly as possible. I was beginning to quiver inside. "If we don't want to go up on top, do we still want to stay here?"

"No," Alex immediately responded.

Methodically, we were fighting our terror and the unseen danger by trying to have a calm, rational conversation. I knew that if we gave in to our panic and tried to flee, things would only get worse. I continued my forced calm.

"Well, if we don't want to go up on top and we don't want to stay here, then we don't have to stay here, do we?"

"No," Alex replied.

"Then lets go!" I said, immediately starting in the direction of the pickup truck.

We began striding toward perceived safety 75 yards to the west. My legs were starting to shake as I walked. I did not want to be the last guy off that bridge. If we were going to be attacked, I wanted to face whatever it was rather than be grabbed by it from behind. Besides, Alex is bigger than me. He is 6'3" and is 240 pounds of muscle. I am just a mere 6'1" and 205 pounds. I felt a little more confident knowing that he was directly behind me covering my backside. However, the other, more important reason that I wanted to go first was that I was finally catching on to what was happening to us. We were under sudden, intense, powerful, violent demonic attack and I knew what I had to do.

An unseen but nonetheless real, violent swirling of evil spirits was issuing from the clearing in the woods. I also sensed evil radiating toward us from the old mill to the south of us. We were being swarmed by a frenzy of evil the same way piranhas or killer bees overwhelm hapless animals that stumble into their domain. The air was swirling all around us, filled with fathomless hatred. Our insides were also filling up with the powerful, unfiltered violence. I was having difficulty maintaining control of my mind, my thoughts, my feelings, my body. Very violent and graphic three-dimensional images were exploding through my mind. One moment I am being skewered with a sword, the next I am being shredded by knives and claws. It was nearly overwhelming.

It was difficult to pray because it was very difficult to maintain rational, coherent thought in the midst of the evil onslaught. But pray I did. First I claimed the Blood of Christ Jesus over both Alex and myself. Second I began praying for Christ to protect us, to be with us, and to make the evil go away. Third, I was praying directly at the evil, rebuking it in the name and authority of

Jesus Christ.

I set the pace as we strode back to the pickup truck. I wanted to get out of there as quickly as possible but I continued resisting the urge to run, knowing that our strategic retreat would then turn into a rout and all hope would be lost. They wanted us to panic because then they could control the rhythm of the attack. In a flash of *my* thought, I thanked God for having reassured me an hour earlier of His infinite love for me. I knew, as clearly as I am aware of gravity, that He was with us and would somehow protect and deliver us. God had prepared me for this unexpected, vicious attack. It was also because of His mercy and love for Alex that He had prepared me.

As we walked the tracks back to where our truck was parked, we had to walk through a gauntlet of demons that had lined our path. The presence of the demons was increasing from the moment that we first heard the metallic clink a few minutes earlier. I knew without a doubt that if we did not leave the area, the demons would fully materialize from the spiritual world. With each step toward the truck their figures and faces were becoming more visible, more tangible like a fade-in in a movie. We could see and sense robed and hooded beings that were horribly grotesque. Some were frighteningly disfigured, others had no faces but exuded ugliness. I was praying without pause.

It was a continuous struggle for the control of my mind, my thoughts, and my feelings. Once or twice I began to have the false fear that Alex had turned into a demon or that he had been overcome. I quickly glanced backward to be certain he was still with me. I did not want to lose him. I could see in his face that he, too, was struggling to maintain control. We were in very real and immediate danger. Every fiber or atom in our beings was electrified with terror and unfiltered violence within and without. It was a long, frightening walk back to the truck.

We finally reached the pickup truck. I did not stop praying. We were outnumbered and would have been overpowered had we not had the presence of God with us whether directly or through angels loyal to the Most High.

The truck was unlocked. We both climbed in immediately upon finally reaching it, and locked the doors. In the glare of the interior dome light, I really could see that Alex was just as terrorized as I was. Fear, confusion, alarm, and urgency were plainly seen in his face and actions. He inserted the truck key into the ignition and cranked it. The truck didn't start. Perhaps Alex had momentarily flooded the engine or perhaps it was simply because the pickup was a couple years old. I worried that the demons had somehow caused it to not start. I prayed for the engine to start. I did not want to have to get out and walk. I wasn't certain we would survive.

As I sat in the cab of the pickup, I could "see" demons standing just on the otherside of the passenger door window, thrusting spears at me. Another one thrust a chain saw at me. They seemed to know my personal fears as well as general human fears. Thankfully, no evil was inside the truck cab. It was just on the other side of the glass. The cab seemed to be our sanctuary space. I desperately wanted to drive out of the area. I knew we would be in trouble if we had to walk out. It was just us and them with no human civilization around for a mile or two in the moonlit night. I kept praying while Alex continued cranking the engine. We had to drive out of there. Finally the engine started.

"Alex, take your time driving out of here. I don't want to get stuck here."

He didn't reply. He simply began turning the truck around and proceeding back toward the paved road in a deliberate but prompt manner. We reached the road and headed west across the valley floor. I sensed spirits following us for a few moments like angry bees. They ceased chasing us as we drove farther away and as I continued to pray.

After a few minutes, we began talking about what had just happened. I was a serious follower of Christ whereas Alex was more of an agnostic. Thus I viewed him as the "control group". That is, I had a framework, if not a bias, of Christian knowledge and meaning to conclude that what had just happened was a demonic attack. Alex did not necessarily have to understand the event the way I quickly did. However, before I could share my thoughts, Alex spoke.

"I guess its true what they say about that place."

"What's that?" I asked.

"Well, people say that back there in the woods people worship the devil."

A shiver ran through me but I was also strangely pleased because that confirmed what I had concluded about the experience. I was also irritated with my friend.

"Alex, if I knew that, I would never have gone to the bridge!" Continuing, I said, "You know, as bad as it was right where we were, the strongest anger or violence seemed to be coming from the old mill farther down the river."

"The mill is where people say they do the animal sacrifices."

"Alex, I was praying like a maniac once I realized what was going on."

We both agreed that it was a terrifying experience. Importantly, our experiences were identical in what we thought, felt, and saw, including the conviction that if we did not flee from the bridge and train tracks, the evil beings would fully materialize. He and I finished each other's sentences as we briefly shared what each of us experienced and saw. This reassured me that it was not a product of my Christianized imagination. It was such a disturbing and weird event that part of me wanted to deny it as being real. I asked Alex if he wanted to join me as I continued praying.

"Now that you've experienced hell, would you like to pray to God?"

Continued prayer was necessary as I still felt anger and hatred being beamed at us from the demons. I also wanted to ensure that no spiritual wounds or doors in us had been opened that could cause problems for us such as depression, hardening of our hearts toward God, or oppression.

"Sure," Alex said without hesitation.

Before starting, I briefly shared basic Christian concepts regarding the struggle between good and evil. I explained my belief in the central role of Jesus Christ in this mysterious, mostly unseen, cosmic, transreality war. That the basic way of avoiding hell and obtaining eternal life is through conscious surrendering or offering of a person's will and life back to God. As we prayed, God's presence filled the pickup truck cab. Alex became aware of peace, joy, lightness of being, and an illumination or glow filling the truck cab.

"Alex, tonight you have experienced both heaven and hell. Few people ever experience both so directly, especially in the same day. I hope that you do not forget what happened here tonight."

Despite my hopes and prayers, later that night vivid dreams and nightmares woke me up several times. Whether still in a "dream" as well as when I woke up, I claimed the Blood of Christ and commanded the spirits to leave me alone in the name of Jesus Christ. Each time, after a few minutes, the evil would leave.

A lasting result of that night on the bridge is that I have a heightened sensitivity to evil, both spiritual and human. Humans generate a lot of evil without help. Yet, from time to time, I also sense a deeper, stronger dimension to a person's anger, hatred, abuse of power, or corruption that is a spiritual evil or energy animating and guiding the person. Humans truly do seem to be vessels in which evil or Holiness can dwell. Many people seem to be empty or neutral or dim; neither evil nor holy. Others are struggling to grow and to be filled with the Holy Spirit. Still others clearly have evil to varying degrees. The experience on the train bridge and tracks that night makes me question the intelligence and wisdom of people who worship spiritual evil. Far more common are those of us who simply play or toy with it. Playing with evil is as easy and seemingly innocent as being involved in astrology, consulting psychics, playing certain games, or using Tarot cards.

I will always be grateful to God for His faithful love for me and Alex. He didn't have to make a point of revealing Himself to me immediately before we went to the bridge. A guilty conscience would have sufficed to end my temporary rebellion that night. In addition, the events of that night make it difficult for me to think that He doesn't know what is going on in the world or with me in the present and in the future. In fact, I do believe that He knows what will happen to us and within us long before we even get to a specific "place" in space-time.

I still suffer, make mistakes, and struggle at times in my daily life but I live with the confident trust that He loves people, that He is present in our world (actually it is His), and that He is involved in our lives, especially if we invite Him in. This reduces the sting or fear in life, making it easier to be a better person. I am not on my own in an indifferent or hostile universe with an impotent or absent god.

Chapter 11
Bless Your Home

As part of my life change in late August 1977, I asked the rector (head priest) from our church to come to my family's house to bless it. There was accumulated hatred and anger in our house. The people who live in a home and the quality of their emotional, mental, and spiritual health creates and contributes to the "spirit" or energy of the house. Fr. MacKinnon and I walked through my home holding candles representing the light of Christ, reciting prayers, and sprinkling holy water in each room and area. As we did this, I heard or sensed viscious, ugly screams coming from unseen crowds of demonic beings. It was very disturbing. I prayed to them to repent and return to Jesus. I prayed to God to bless them. I then sensed confusion and hatred coming from them toward me. But they all left my home. As we walked through each room, asking Jesus and His Holy Spirit to drive out evil and to dwell there, an oppression or bad feeling left the room, replaced by a feeling of lightness and light. When we finished, I thanked Fr. MacKinnon for coming out to bless our home.

While we were blessing my family's home, part of me felt a little silly, like I was participating in some kind of superstitious ritual. I wondered what the neighbors might have thought if they happened to see Fr. MacKinnon entering our home. But the better part of me knew that I should bless my family's home because I wanted to live in close union with God. Our home needed to be cleansed, as much as possible, of all that is not of His Spirit.

A home filled with the Holy Spirit is a peaceful and restful home. Having it blessed is the ultimate Feng Shui that is usually disregarded. Feng Shui is an ancient Chinese practice that is concerned with proper placement of furniture and rooms within properly oriented structures such as homes; believed to optimize energy flow, thus increases a peaceful environment, in addition to other benefits. A blessed home is a place where God feels comfortable inhabiting, an island of solace in our troubled world. It is similar to entering a church and immediately feeling a welcoming peace and calm stillness. It is due to the Holy Spirit dwelling there. It is the opposite of a haunted house or a site where gruesome murders or devil worship or other evils have occurred. I believe that every person who truly desires to live in union with God should have their home and even their places of business blessed by holy Christians, whether priests, pastors, or lay persons.

Spirit-filled followers of Jesus Christ, Spirit-filled churches, Spirit-filled homes and businesses are springs of God's fresh, living waters flowing into our parched world. This is in contrast to the spiritual sewage of evil that rises up into our world bringing death, dis-ease, and suffering of all sorts. Our world desperately needs more springs and vessels of the living waters of Christ.

LEAPS OF FAITH

The Stirring Whisper

The shifting montage of color, light, and wind
drifts gently across the sky.

Teasing me
inviting me
calling me

to drift
to wander

to places I've known
and to places that I should know.

The shifting montage of color, light, and wind
drifts gently across my heart.

Promising me
reminding me
not to forget

that there is community in other places.....

Chapter 12

Time to Move

During Spring Semester 1979 I realized that in order for me to continue growing, healing, and becoming more myself, I had to leave the Chicago area. I had to get away from my family and my past. While you cannot avoid your past by running, it is just as true that moving to a new locale can alter the issues and influences of your past, placing them at arm's length. This allows you to look at them in new light, often making it easier to change and grow.

I, of course, prayed about this decision. I was very excited to know that the Holy Spirit was urging me to leave Illinois. I didn't know where I was going yet but my thirst for adventure had been aroused. Five conditions or factors emerged as a sort of checklist or matrix to find the correct place that I needed to move to. Those five criteria were: (1) wherever I was to go, it had to be far away from home; (2) it had to be in or near the mountains; (3) mild winters; (4) the university or college had to offer biophysics; and (5) it had to be some place I had never been to before.

In late April 1979, I thought that Texas would be a good destination to plug into my decision matrix. I knew that Texas was closer to mountains than Illinois and that they have mild winters. I had never lived in or traveled to Texas before, either. It was far from home. What schools might offer biophysics? I reviewed a copy of Barron's College Guide turning to the Texas section. Trinity University in San Antonio offered biophysics. Continuing to pray about the decision, I booked a flight to San Antonio. I stayed a couple of days. Despite the fun I was having with my student hosts, and despite learning about Trinity's excellent biophysics and pre-med program, it was not the correct choice. I liked it but the Holy Spirit did not. I was clearly getting a "No" signal. This troubled and confused me. I needed to leave Illinois. I had to know where I was going as soon as possible because I needed to apply to whichever university was in that new locale quickly as the beginning of Summer Break 1979 was just a couple weeks away. I worried that I might miss the chance to start Fall Semester in the new place.

By the third week of May, Spring Semester at Trinity College in Deerfield, Illinois ended. I had been too busy finishing my classes to give much thought regarding where I was to move. On that first Saturday morning after the end of Spring Semester Finals Week, I woke up and just sat on my bed. I asked God where I could go, where I should move to.

Oregon popped into my head. I thought about it for a moment and said, "Why not?" Oregon fit the first four criteria for my move. I got my copy of the Barron's Guide off my bedroom desk and sat back down on my bed. I turned to the Oregon section of the guide. I scanned the list looking for which schools might offer biophysics. I stopped at Oregon State University (OSU). It offered biophysics. I got excited because I had suddenly discovered where I was to probably move to.

I continued praying about the choice of Oregon. The response was consistently positive — at least there was no "catch" or negative feeling like when you run your hand along a piece of smooth wood and catch a splinter in your hand. It was smooth all the way each time I thought about it. Nothing was forced, it was an easy peace about the choice.

It was exciting to realize that God is so cool as to guide me to a place as wonderful as Oregon. Up to this point, I guess I hadn't thought of God as being a truly wonderful, kind, and even cool Being. Until then He was more simply a powerful authority who loved me and protected me but always seemed somewhat formal and distant in an indefinable way. In retrospect, it was a turning point. More of a revelation on my part and not so much a change in Him, it led to a more intimate and familial relationship with the Father of all spirits, all things, all places, and all times. I moved closer by a deeper and less guarded trust in Him as He had in a way made Himself more vulnerable or open to me.

I had originally thought of Oregon because Trinity College (which I was attending when I realized I had to move) had a college extension program at Lincoln Commons in southern Oregon. As well, I discovered that a friend of mine, Fr. O'Leary, had graduated from OSU in Corvallis years before. As before, there was not just continuity in my life and decisions, it appeared that there was planned continuity. This contributes to the deepest sort of integrity, true integration, of a person's being.

I quickly applied to OSU and was just as promptly accepted. I numbered the days on my calendar for the summer. I prepared for the move, saving money from my summer factory job and saying good-bye to people and places that had been a part of my life up to that point. I studied maps and read back-issues of National Geographic magazine to plan a quick sight-seeing tour of the state of Oregon. Soon I would be on my way to a new life and new adventures that I could not even begin to imagine!

Absolutely, without a doubt, moving to Oregon and living there for the three years that I did was a strategic time in my life, in my becoming. I would not be who I am today without having lived there first. To follow the God revealed and shared through Jesus Christ does not mean an abdication of my reasoning, my analytical gifts, and to act irrationally. No, what it means is that I am challenged and urged to use all that I have been given in my creation and development to prayerfully discern the will of God, trusting that He will faithfully provide guidance that leads us to greater, fuller life. What a great way to live.

Chapter 13
The Great Craftsman

Once I learned of my acceptance to Oregon State University (OSU), I numbered the days on my calendar. Summer 1979 was spent waiting, anticipating, and planning. The shedding of my current life and the discovery of a new one was ever present in my mind and heart no matter what I did for the 75 or 80 days until mid-August when I would move out west. During that time I said good-bye to people and places around the Chicago area that I had known for the past nine years. When it was time for me to leave, I was ready. The only glitch was that the bank where I had my summer savings account had withdrawal restrictions that I learned about at the last minute before leaving for Oregon. I would have to close my account in stages over a couple of weeks. I would not be starting my new life with all of the money I had planned on.

I headed out to Oregon with a friend, Michael, who was going to the Trinity College campus extension program at Lincoln Commons in southern Oregon. However, we amicably parted ways in Pierre, South Dakota on the morning of the third day because it was clear to both of us that we did not share the same spirit or rhythm for the trip. I hadn't clearly realized it before we started out, but the trip was a very important catharsis for me. We planned to meet again at Lincoln Commons in four or five days. He would take a bus out to there and I would deliver his belongings he packed for his semester of study.

By the time I reached the Pacific Ocean three days later, I was a new man. Like sailing from one hemisphere to another, I had acquired an entirely new set of orientation points by which to guide my life. Gone were my family, the limiting perceptions of me held by others, and the constant topographical reminders of my old, self-destructive, and miserable life. Now I had the ocean, two mountain ranges, and all sorts of new, unknown people to experience and explore. An entirely new world of ideas and philosophies was about to unfold before me, both in and out of college. I was ecstatic. Familiar songs on the radio sounded new, almost exotic. "My Sharona", "Rise", "Don't Bring Me Down", and other songs are indelibly associated with this time in my life.

I first arrived in Corvallis about three weeks before the start of Fall Term '79. I stopped at Westminster House, the campus Episcopalian student center. I introduced myself and temporarily stored some of my belongings in their basement. I mailed another withdrawal slip back to the bank in Lake Zurich, Illinois using Westminster House as a temporary address. I then headed down to Lincoln Commons, located approximately 20 winding miles or so east of Ashland, Oregon, in the Cascade Mountains. I needed to deliver Michael's belongings to him and to visit with some former classmates and a couple of professors whom I had known at Trinity the previous academic school year.

After spending a few days with the group, we parted ways in the coastal town of Coos Bay. Their short excursion up the coast was complete so they turned east to return to Lincoln Commons. I continued north along the coast on Highway 101, heading toward Corvallis. I needed to return to secure off-campus housing and to register for the Fall Term.

A couple hours later I was leaning against the side of my car gazing out over the ocean. It was beautiful, as was the view in either direction up and down the coast. In a few hours, the day would be on the horizon, flashing a beautiful sunset as it disrobed. The problem was that despite the surrounding beauty and the fabulous time I was having, despite my celebration of freedom and new life, I only had an eighth of a tank of gas remaining, I was out of money, and I was still about 75 - 80 miles and one mountain range from Corvallis. When I decided to drive down to Ashland to visit the college extension, I hadn't planned on the short trip across northern California to the coast before heading north again.

Going over mountains burns more gas than driving on flat-land. No matter how I looked at it, I simply did not have enough gasoline to make it back to Westminster House. Earlier in the day I spent time explaining to God how people need money while on earth and that cars run on gas. I asked for His help. I figured if He could feed 5,000 people with just a couple of loaves of bread and some fish, He could stretch my gas if He so willed. So far He had not done so.

I pulled over because I was at a crucial decision point. I had enough remaining gasoline for about 30 - 40 more miles. Perhaps I could drive "somewhere" within that estimated range and try to pick up an odd job for some cash. Unfortunately, I had no idea where "somewhere" might be. I didn't know anybody who could help me. I was all alone except for God, and I wasn't really certain if He was going to help me or not. So there I was.

Suddenly a car pulled off the road and stopped next to mine. It was a coast range hippie, with his common law wife, and their two kids in a small, late model car. He got out and ambled over to me.

"Hey. Do you have a light?" he asked.

"Ya, sure. Say, could I bum one from you?" I replied. I don't smoke but I was stressed and wanted to join him in the social ceremony of a shared smoke.

"Sure," he said.

We both lit up and stood there gazing out over the cliff watching the sun tuck into the horizon as the ocean splashed against the rocks below. After a moment, we began talking.

"Something bugging you, man?" he asked.

I explained my predicament. He introduced himself and suggested that I follow him and his family back to their place for BBQ oysters. He told me that he could give me some money in a couple of days because he was expecting to get paid shortly from a job he had. I offered to work for it but he refused, saying that he would simply give me some gas money.

"Well, that's weird," I said. "I was just standing here praying about what I should do. Why'd you pull over?"

"It just looked like you could use someone to talk to, like you had something on your mind. Besides, I needed a light for my cigarette."

I thought about his offer for a moment, saying a quick, silent prayer. Nothing inside told me "NO", so I said yes to his offer.

An hour or so later I was helping light the campfire on which the oysters were to be cooked in a meadow next to a small river. We used knives and a screw driver to pry open the oysters. I was using my Buck hunting knife. It was an eight inch sheath knife of hardened steel. Buck knives are renowned for their strength and ability to keep an edge. Thus I was very surprised and kind of upset when I chipped off the very tip of it shucking an oyster. Less than an eighth of an inch was missing but its appearance was forever marred.

That night I slept in an old broken down van while they slept in their converted school bus RV. I was still praying to God asking for help and for protection too. I thought it was kind of odd that these people had stopped to talk to me just when I was praying for help and trying to figure out how to solve my problem. I was wondering if God had sent them my way or if He had anything to do with it at all.

The following morning I awoke to a beautiful day. Oregon in the late summer, before the rains begin, is exquisite. The hippie and his wife left for their day jobs, dropping their two children off at a local school nearby. I was alone with their two dogs. To help pass the time I decided to go hiking. I was about three miles inland from the coast next to a small river that flowed into an estuary at the coast. The dirt access road that ran east from Hwy. 101 into the Coast Range more or less followed the river and the meandering meadow that lay next to it. There were other homesteads here and there up the dirt road. I decided to cross the river and hike up the mountains on the other side by following deer paths through the scrub. I crossed the little river walking on a large tree that had fallen across it. The dogs followed me across. I was wearing my sheath knife.

While hiking, I had the specific thought that I really did not need it anymore for protection because I had become a man of peace. I had specifically purchased it for the move out west, as well as for camping. However, I now believed that God would protect me from any harm or violence that might threaten me. Yet I could not just throw the knife away. It was a good knife and it had cost approximately $40. I wasn't certain what to do with it. Meanwhile my mind wandered onto other things.

The next day was pretty much the same. Again, the hippie family left for the day, leaving me to wait alone. I was waiting for the hippie to get paid and give me some gas money as he had promised. I again offered to do some work in exchange for the money but he made it clear that he would just make it a gift. I only needed $7 - 10 dollars in gas to get back to Corvallis.

That second night was strange. There was growing tension and mild hostility from the hippie and his wife toward me. In retrospect, I think that part of the problem was that his wife viewed me as an unwanted guest hanging around waiting for some of *their* sparse money. I resented this impression because her "husband" invited me to stay with them for a couple days, promising to give me gas money even though I offered to work for it. Also, an anger was welling up inside the man. I could feel it and it troubled or worried me. I felt as if he wanted to triumph over me in some fashion. I did not know why, but I sensed a rivalry. Maybe it was because I told him of my excitement to begin classes at OSU while he was sort of stuck in his lifestyle. However, the conflict seemed deeper. It was as if there was a contest between his belief system and my God: Who or What was real, accurate, and relevant to living life as a human being.

The differences in our faith orientations were becoming clear. I have never been one to trumpet my faith or to wear my religion on my sleeve. I prefer to live and act it, then maybe say something. It is always irritating whenever I encounter "trumpeting" or self-righteousness in other people, whatever their religion might be. No one has all of the answers on anything. Smugness is not the same as holiness. I must have told them that I was trying to follow Christ in my life. They professed adherence to the Urantia Foundation teachings combined with the typical hippie approach to reality which is "create your own truth" mix and match subjectivity just as long as it doesn't demand too much morally, a lazy anarchy. The primary set of Urantia teachings is contained in a four inch thick volume. It is a set of teachings revealed by an angel to a guy early in the 20th Century that provides instruction on the formation and structure of the universe; the purpose of life; eternity and its entrance requirements; as well as the origins and purpose of Jesus Christ (somehow the Church's teachings including the Bible got it wrong). It is not Christianity, although in fairness, a person might awaken a curiosity about Christ initially through Urantia before becoming orthodox in their beliefs and behavior. God can find anybody, even if we cannot always find God.

After dinner we played backgammon, as we had the night before. Only this night he was saying some angry and bad things about the Holy Spirit. It seemed that he had a degree of hatred toward Jesus and His Holy Spirit. I felt uncomfortable with the situation but remained calm and alert.

It is one thing to critique or even ridicule religious custom and practice. Everyone is entitled to their opinion and certainly every religion can benefit from balanced criticism as needed. It is an entirely different matter, however, to denigrate or denounce the Holy Spirit. Jesus seems to be tolerant of our insults and anger for the sake of winning our hearts. But even God has His limits. Attacking His Holy Spirit is dumber and more dangerous than licking an electric fence. The Holy Spirit should be on everyone's short list of people not to anger (such as the state trooper who pulls you over, the cook preparing your meal, your wife on a Friday before a three day weekend, and so forth). But where was I going to go on a sixteenth of a tank of gas at night 20 - 30 miles from the closest small town? I prayed a lot that night. I was praying for him because of what he was saying as well as for myself and my situation. I needed God to be with me. Something amazing that was also disturbing occurred while we played backgammon. I won the dice roll to go first. I rolled perfect dice each time such that he never got all of his pieces out of my area before I got all of mine completely off the board to win the game. For most of the game, he could not move any of his pieces because I was blocking his moves perfectly. I whooped him without even trying. I have never played a game as brilliant since that one. I became increasingly embarrassed with each perfect roll of the dice. It is not polite to crush your host in a game, but on the other hand, I could not purposely "throw" the game either. I continued to make the best moves possible with each roll, all the while hoping that my "luck" with the dice would change so I could lose without it being obvious.

Both he and I felt a very strong presence that I knew to be the Holy Spirit. It was as if the Holy Spirit was playing backgammon against the man, determining the dice rolls. I was merely throwing the dice and moving the pieces. The Holy Spirit's presence became so strong that it clearly unnerved him. While I was just feeling a little spooked by the end of the game, he was very angry and agitated. His wife came out of the sleeping quarters at the end of the bus and directed him to go to bed with her. They left me sitting there. After a moment, I went to my spot in the other vehicle and fell asleep, praying for safety and for gas money.

When I awoke the next morning, they had already left for their daily activities. I felt uneasy all day. I knew that I had to leave but was very uncertain of my next move. I no longer felt safe or welcome. Yet I was no better off than I had been when the hippie first asked me for a "light" two days earlier. I felt as if I had wasted my time staying with them, that it was a mistake.

By the time I anxiously decided to leave, it was late afternoon. I had to hurry so I would not be around when they returned home. I threw my sleeping bag into my car and left their homestead campsite in the meadow. I drove back down the dirt road toward Highway 101. On the way I passed by the hippie's other car that had recently broken down. I had driven past it on the way in to their current "homestead" area. I was certain it had gas that I could siphon into my tank. I backed my Cutlass up to his car, end-to-end. I opened my trunk and took out a siphon.

I was about to set it up when I stopped what I was doing. I had been trying to convince myself that it was not only OK to take gas out of his non-working car but that it was the intelligent thing to do. Afterall, the hippie had promised to give me some money for gas, so he owed me. Besides, this car of his wasn't driveable so it did not need gas. I was in a survival situation. The first rule of survival is that there are no rules — just survive. Being resourceful, taking advantage of your surroundings is the way to survive. However, a sudden single thought caused me to stop this line of thinking and to end my siphoning intentions. I had bumped into the second rule of survival: pray.

"How can God save me if I do not give Him a chance to do so?" I wondered.

To siphon gas or to steal is to cheat God and myself out of an opportunity for Him to help me in a clean or direct manner. It seemed that it would be a great lack of faith on my part. What good is a god that you have to lie, cheat, and steal for to make him, her, or it seem real? Thinking these thoughts, I put my siphon away. I got back into my car and started it. I began driving away from my last tangible hope of getting back to Corvallis in my lifetime.

"OK. If You're God, do something! I call upon the name of the Lord Jesus Christ. Save me! If You are really real and You want me to believe in You, do something, help me. Please!"

Moments later, almost back to Highway 101, the hippie family passed me on their way home just about a mile from where I was going to siphon their gasoline from their other car. I was immediately grateful that they would not see me siphoning gas out of their broken-down car. The situation would have been ugly.

When I reached the highway, I decided to head north again toward the cutoff road heading east over the mountains to Corvallis. It was about 25 miles north in the coastal town of Waldport. I barely had enough gas to reach Waldport. I was asking God to help me, reminding Him that I had just put all my trust in Him to get me out of the bind I was in. I wasn't nagging or whining to Him. I was just urgent and intense.

I thought that perhaps I could sell some of my personal belongings to get money to buy gas. After a moment I decided that I could try to sell my knife. It was perfect. I could get rid of my knife in exchange for the money that I needed to buy gasoline. Wondering what price I should try to sell it for, the figure of $10 popped into my head. It seemed very fair. It was a $40 knife with a chipped point. Pricing the knife at $10 was pricing it to sell hopefully easily.

A few minutes later I drove into Waldport, population under 1000. It was 5:45 PM. I saw an open gas station. Pulling in, I parked in front of one of the pumps. I walked into the station, taking my sheathed knife with me. There was a police car parked in front. I pitched the only attendant on duty, explaining my situation. He told me that I was lucky to be talking to him because he was closing in 15 minutes and he was the only gas station within 30 miles. Although he listened to my persuasive plea for help, he didn't really want to buy the knife. Instead he directed me toward the two police officers who were standing in the service area. I hesitated but the attendant assured me that the cops were OK guys. At this time in my life, I had shoulder length hair and was growing my beard back. I was concerned about getting hassled from small town cops. I walked over to the interior doorway that connects the cashier area with the service bays.

"Uh, scuse me. Sir? Would you be interested in buying my Buck knife for ten dollars? I'm out of money and gas and I have to drive back to Corvallis."

"No thanks. I'm not interested in it. But maybe my partner

is. Ask him," the first police officer said. "Hey Don. This guy wants to know if you want to buy a knife."

I was hopeful but nervous. This next cop was my last chance — at least for that day — to get back to Corvallis. Officer Don walked into the front lobby area from the service bays. One of their cars was in for periodic servicing.

"Sir, your partner suggested that I ask you if you would like to buy my Buck knife. I need money to buy gas to get back to Corvallis."

"Can I see it?" Don asked.

I handed him the sheathed knife. Don removed it from the sheath and inspected it closely.

"The point is chipped," he said.

"I know. That's why I'm selling it for just $10 which is a very fair price. It is a perfectly good $40 Buck knife aside from the slightly chipped point. I no longer want it and I need gas money to get back to Corvallis."

After another moment of thinking about it while holding the knife, the officer said that he would buy it.

"You know, I have always wanted a Buck General but never bought one because of the price. It seemed too expensive. But I like to hunt and this will be a good knife for that," Don said.

Officer Don then pulled a paycheck for exactly $10.00 out of one of his shirt pockets where he had put it earlier that day.

"Its funny because I got this check today for some overtime work I did for the county a month ago. I thought I had been paid everything for it already," Don said. "Bob, can you cash this for me so I can buy the knife?"

"Sure. No problem," Bob the service station attendant said.

Don endorsed the back of the check, gave it to Bob, Bob put it in the cash drawer, and handed me a ten dollar bill.

I was ecstatic. I told them my story. We were all struck by the perfect seamlessness of the event. I pumped eight dollars of gasoline into my car, giving me close to half of a tank. I pocketed two dollars cash. I drove back to Corvallis singing praises to

God all the way. God had answered my prayers in an incredible manner!

God truly is a craftsman, intimately involved in the minutiae of our daily lives — especially if we invite Him in when He knocks at the door of our hearts. Or in this case, to get out of the boat and walk on water to Him.

It will always impress me how He wove together various threads of space-time, filled with separate and independently willed people and events, like woolen threads of an oriental rug, to create an intricate and beautiful pattern to the benefit of all involved. He planned and prepared each thread. He ministered and witnessed to several humans of His holiness, love, omniscience, and participation in our lives.

Only God can plan, prepare, and deliver like this consistently. It is wonderful and exciting. Having this faith transforms the struggle and fear in my life, giving me courage. With inward courage I am ready to live. Life with the Great Craftsman is not always easy but it is deeply rewarding and life giving, hopefully even eternal.

Chapter 14

Limits to Faith; Limits in Faith

In late October 1985 I suddenly became aware of a limit to my faith when I was attacked by a barroom buddy who snapped one night. "David" was a deeply troubled Viet Nam vet. The war probably just exacerbated pre-existing difficulties, but war is deeply traumatic for many, many men. It was that inner disturbance, the threat of violence mixed in with shattered woundedness, that interested me.

As a boy in Ohio, one of my friends had a father who was a World War II (WW II) veteran. He was confined to a wheel chair and had a metal plate in his head. He had his good days and he had frequent "bad days". I was not allowed in their house on Chris' father's bad days. In fact, there were several people in our Middleburg Heights, Ohio neighborhood who carried deep scars and fears from WW II and the Korean War too. The German family on our street was so secretive, with paranoid hostility. In retrospect, I concluded that they were probably Nazi sympathizers. There were Italian immigrant families that had been traumatized by WW II and Mussolini. Other families were American but had lost their sons in the "Big War". They had little shrines in their windows or in their living rooms to their lost sons and husbands.

At the same time, the Viet Nam War was hitting full stride on our TV sets. Some of the older brothers of my friends in the neighborhood were drafted. I still have a Louisville Slugger baseball bat from one guy who bought several of them that he handed out to several of us kids as something to remember him by. I remember that he seemed excited about going off to war. When he returned a year or so later, I never saw him very much, unlike before he left for the war. The few times that I happened to catch a glimpse of him in his family's driveway, he seemed quieter, not very outgoing anymore.

Thus, I was interested in getting to know the guy sitting on the barstool next to me at the Blue Moon Tavern on 45th Street in Seattle. Now I could perhaps get some answers to my questions about why many Viet Nam vets seemed so troubled long after the war. As well, I wanted to share the healing energies of Christ with him if possible, that is, if he was interested.

The night David snapped, we were having fun hanging out, talking and goofing around while drinking beer. I left the bar in search of him after I realized that he was missing for several minutes. I walked two blocks over to the house where he rented a room in a house that one of his friends, Randy, owned.

I found David hurriedly grabbing his belongings out of the garage behind the house and throwing them into the back of his late model Chevy pick-up truck. He seemed agitated. He ignored me as I strolled back to the garage apron area. I tossed a greeting toward him and then opened the driver's side door of his pick-up truck and sat down on the bench seat. The motor was idling.

He strode quickly over to me.

"Dave. Come on! Lets keep the party going. Lets go to a different bar!" I said.

He tried to pull me out of the truck. I thought it was just the friendly "wrasslin'" that guys sometimes do. So I "wrassled" back, effectively shoving him off me, wresting free of his frantic gripping.

As he stepped back from the pick-up truck cab, he snatched an axe from the truck bed where he had put it minutes earlier. He took a couple steps backward and stopped. He drew the axe up, holding the axe head up with his left hand, and the handle butt with his right hand. I got out of the idling truck and stood squarely in front of him. It dawned on me that David was really angry with me! I asked him what his problem was. His response was mostly angry, incoherent gibberish. Apparently, I had accidentally and innocently said something to his friend Randy that fit a larger pattern in a deteriorating relationship between David and Randy. David had run out of the bar in search of Randy to try to placate him. Randy responded by kicking David out. This is why David was hurriedly loading his truck.

Suddenly, as we continued talking, he swung the axe at me. I saw it happen in slow motion like seeing a snow ball out of the corner of your eye just before it hits you. He struck my left knee as hard as he could. He was trying to chop my knee, presumably with murderous intent to do more once he knocked me down to the ground. Being a landscaper, he knew how to accurately swing the axe just as a baseball player knows how and when to swing a bat to connect with a ball.

Amazingly he missed! The axe handle just below the blade slammed against the inner side of my left knee. The blade cut through my jeans, making a shallow gash across my calf muscle. Thank God I did not move as I saw him swing the axe. Had things been different even just by an inch, "I would not be standing here today."

The moment he struck me, I felt a flash of surprise, then a flash of fear, a flash of intense anger, then total peace as God made His presence known to me, and perhaps to David, too. A flash of shock and disbelief momentarily relaxed his angry face. I had been shaken, then stirred. I immediately began praying for help as I looked for a way out of the situation. Once again, my guardian angel was working overtime. At the same time, David wrenched the axe head off from behind my knee, further cutting me.

I immediately began walking backwards, away from the truck, down the driveway, toward the street 100 feet away. There was no way I was going to turn my back and run. He was following me just four or five feet away from me, with the axe drawn up again into striking position. I decided that I would control the pace of our deadly dance, and thereby exercise some control over this crazy situation. With each step backward, I carefully and deliberately placed a foot on the ground at a sure and

123

steady pace. Just after he hit me with the axe, I put my left hand into my left jeans pocket. In my left pocket was a martial arts butterfly knife. It is a four inch blade that can be flipped out and set for striking or slashing in the blink of an eye. David knew I had it because, coincidentally, I had shown it to him earlier in the evening at the bar.

Suddenly, for the first time in my life, I had to make a choice as to whether I would kill another person. I thought about doing it several times as I walked backward down his driveway. I repeatedly visualized my lunge and plunge attack, in rehearsal like an athlete before a competition. If I was going to do it, I did not want to telegraph it to David. It had to be a quick, smooth, fluid motion if I was to be victorious. Indeed, had he continued to attack I probably would have whipped out the knife to protect myself. However, I did not have too. I got away safely and have never seen him since.

Importantly, I still pray for him on occasion. I pray for his peace, that he does not harm anyone else, and that somehow his attack on me was like the lancing of an infectious boil of pain, hatred and violence. Perhaps God was able to draw off some of his sickness, helping him begin to heal if he wanted to do so.

Among the many things I learned from the attack, I now unequivocally understand that there are limits to what prayer and friendship can accomplish, at least in a short time span. No more empathetic stupidity for me. It is one thing to be a "fool for Christ"; it is another to be an idiot. Sometimes I accommodate others too far or too much. I still find myself doing that even today on occasion.

As well, I reserve my option to kill if I have to. I am not certain if killing is or is not a right, but it certainly is a necessity sometimes. As long as there are dangerously troubled people in the world or rape camps, ethnic "cleansing" and the like, I will always retain that option to kill if necessary. Related to this is the question of whether I would ever be a martyr for my faith. My answer is, "Perhaps." It all depends upon how the Holy Spirit leads me in that hypothetical situation. I am glad that God made His presence known to me immediately when David struck me with the ax. Knowing He was present gave me another response option to the deadly situation. It allowed me to "absorb" the blow without returning violence to my attacker which would have escalated the situation. Put another way, unless God makes it clear to me that I should not be violent to the point of killing to defend myself or my family, I will proceed to do so as is reasonable and necessary to neutralize the threat.

A few years later I found myself in a different kind of situation that was no less serious as it, too, involved attacks on my being. This time however, the struggle was more subtle and prolonged than an ax attack. I worked in a small office with a group of vulgar, dysfunctional people. They hated me for a variety of reasons that can be summed up by the fact that I was not like them. By the second day on the job, I knew that I had made a mistake in accepting the position in that office, that the group was a tight, incestuous clique of spirits and personalities (vulgar, selfish, adulterous, violent, corrupt) opposed to the Spirit in me. I could never fit in, nor accept them as they truly were in contrast to how they presented themselves during the interviews. I wondered how long I would be able to last until I could secure a different job somewhere else. I knew from past experience in similar situations that the best way for me to try to survive and not provoke the wrath of my new coworkers would be to draw myself in tight. "The nail that sticks up gets hit with the hammer." (Japanese proverb). I felt as if God tricked me into taking the job. However, the true and living God is not a deceiver. Thus, I figured, He must have a valuable purpose for having led me into the situation; a purpose that if He told me ahead of time, I may not have agreed to my role in the matter.

Although I instinctively thought about quitting, I didn't for several compelling reasons. For one thing, my wife was just returning to the workforce after having been off work for several months due to her pregnancy and then giving birth to our son.

Money was tight. The next two reasons were business related. A mutual acquaintance in the industry, an influential broker, had referred me to the position, thus I felt a little obligated to stay with the new job in order to not blow any chance of maintaining a business relationship with the broker. As well, my resume was getting a little choppy. I needed to hunker down at one company for awhile. The other key reason that I did not quit immediately was that I had been searching and praying for a different job and this opportunity had fallen into my lap. I prayed during the entire hiring process of three interviews with the manager and with some of my future coworkers. I used my critical reasoning as well as my faith. Based on what the manager told me about the office and where he understood it to be growing, it seemed that I had found a great opportunity. I felt that God had led me to the position, approving of it for me as the next step in my life. I trusted and expected Him to not give me peace if I was jamming my will and perceptions on the choice. If God had something else for me, I trusted that He would lead me differently. For all of these reasons, each equally compelling, I accepted the offer that the manager extended.

For the next 14 months I suffered greatly. The office was very small. There was no place to hide from the tyranny of my coworkers. I had to endure their behavior, attitudes, derogatory treatment, and repulsive racism. My boss was practically a card-carrying member of the Ku Klux Klan. I learned more than I ever wanted to know about female medical problems and farting humor, among other things. I was expected to drink with my boss anytime he wanted to do so, even during the working day. Also, he had one set of rules that we were expected to obey while he had a different, more relaxed set for himself. There was no way to conceal not laughing at many of their jokes or racist comments.

For the record, I still swear on occasion, I hope I always enjoy a drink in the proper circumstances, and on rare occasion I might tell an off-color joke. I am not a stiff, holier-than-thou

Christian who has a narrow and intolerant approach to life on earth. It is God who makes me holy, not me nor anything that I can do. The call to holiness, literally to be set apart, does not preclude getting soiled hands from remaining interactive in the world. Otherwise what use is my "saltness"? I aim to be in the world but not of it. However, I do have my limits. Working in that small office was a bad situation that never improved. The experience pushed me to my limits of health and tested my faith. Like wearing a shoe that is one size too small or rubs your foot in a certain spot, the longer the situation persists, the deeper the pain and suffering that develops from the initial cramped irritation.

In the beginning of the thirteenth month at that company, something profound and powerful happened to me. All along, the personality and behavior of my boss strongly and unexpectedly reminded me of my father. That, in combination with the daily stress and fearful tension of working in the small office, acted like a key or code that unloosed all of the fear, pain, even terror that had been beaten into me verbally, physically, and socially throughout the first half of my life. All of the psychic terror that I gave myself through abuse of psychedelic drugs years earlier also came flooding back.

The release of all of those feelings was overwhelming. For about four or five weeks I felt like I was drowning in terror and pain. It was very confusing and frightening for me. My wife had no idea what was happening inside of me which was both of our faults. I was alone and felt that I might go crazy. I went to the local library to read about delayed stress syndrome because for some reason the thought struck me that my re-feeling and re-experiencing all of the terrible things of my early years and my drug years was a delayed stress release. It helped me to learn that others have suffered in the same way, taking some of the fear out of the process.

I never realized how much terror I carried around deep inside of me until that time in May 1995. I wondered how all of that

127

unconscious pain and terror had colored my life to that point, how it had shaped my personality. Although I became fairly comfortable during the next few months with the entire process of full, deep cleansing and healing, the first two or three weeks were hell.

One night in particular I could not sleep so I got up and began pacing our bedroom. This startled and worried my wife. I was debating, somewhat seriously, whether I should go to the local fire station to get some help in the form of sedatives and a friendly face to talk with. I was running through the possible options in my mind of how to deal with my situation at that moment. All of us have a certain, private sense of solidity, of who we are, of structure, no matter how weak or dis-integrated we may be. However, for me at this time, my structures, my intuitive sense of self "liquefied". I knew that going to the local fire station would be a big mistake because then a serious problem would get blown way out of proportion, that I would lose control and personal power over my own situation. So I went downstairs instead, turned on a light, and began reading the Psalms and praying for help.

My prayers with and to God intensified during this very difficult and frightening time period. Wonderfully, and as I hoped, God "intensified" for me during this time. I became acquainted with the Psalms more closely than I had ever been before. Psalm 27 became my instant favorite. Like an iron lung, it helped me continue breathing, sustaining me while the rest of me healed. Most important, His tangible, undeniable presence intensified for me. It was similar to the recent movie, The Matrix. My everyday programming and sense of balance in this world wobbled, becoming pliant. I again discovered that I could jump off the edge of apparent security into the nothingness of God and be sustained, buoyant. I transcended the regular programming our minds are preset with in order to realize that there is a greater world behind what we normally see and live as real.

In fact, what saved me daily, often hourly, during my entire time in that sick office was my faith and prayer. Prayer not only saved me, it helped me be proactive in fighting back against the hatred and spiritual violence that the four women and two men directed toward me because I was not cut from the same cloth that they were. I fought back by praying for them, for myself, and by continually struggling not to become morbid, defeated, or filled with rage toward them, although it was a repeated temptation. In essence, I rebelled against the situation by exercising my will as I wanted to, not allowing the people or situation to manipulate or possess me.

Most special, at a certain point halfway through my ordeal I became aware of the larger unseen Church of God to which I belong. I sensed many unsolicited prayers for me. Knowing and feeling that I was not alone was like a cool, fresh breeze on a nauseatingly hot, stale day. The experience strengthened and encouraged me, enabling me to continue "turning the other cheek". It renewed my decision and act of will to see the situation out and to continue praying for all of us.

Finally, in mid-June 1995, after a witness of fourteen months (they knew I strive to emulate Jesus), I just walked away one day on a Friday afternoon while taking a break. As I realized that I had just quit the further away I walked, I thought of Rhett Butler turning away from Scarlet at the end of the movie, Gone With The Wind. I was close to my breaking point. I was tired and had enough of working with unhealthy people. Although God had not provided a different job during months of looking on and off, I knew that He already knew when I would walk away when the situation became too toxic for me. I trusted that because He knew that and because of my witness on His behalf to my coworkers, He had another job waiting for me. He did. The following Monday I began working as a contract worker making the same amount of money that I had been earning, only without the persecution, vulgarity, or sickness of coworkers. As with many other times, God had foreseen and provided. Wonderfully and in keeping with His character, God blessed me with deep healing, great growth, and new direction due to my employment at that office.

The greatest blessings that I am aware of include the new direction for my life that was prompted by my job situation and frustrated career (writing); I increased my limits and endurance for suffering and surviving a very hostile environment; and I "discovered" a great friend named Andy who has, among other things, helped and encouraged me to write this book. Also, I in essence had my mid-life crisis a few years earlier than the norm which gives me more time to discover and practice who I really am rather than continuing with less authentic behavior, i.e. doing what my social modeling tells me I should be and do. All of this in addition to the wonderful deep healing inside me. My ocean of pain and sadness was finally drained. Beautiful gardens and farmland now exist where the ocean used to be. Acting with courage and choosing freedom is easier when there is a living God to trust in. God took care of me, as well as other people, in many different ways arising out of my employment at that office.

Working in that office was also a blunt reminder of how we often treat each other. Paraphrasing Abraham Lincoln, most people can endure adversity, that the true test of character is how people behave when they have or think they have power. Realizing that we only exist because of relationship to others and other things, how we relate to each other becomes an urgent matter. I have come to realize that one of the greatest sins we can and do commit is the misuse of power, casually, routinely, as a matter of course in everyday life.

When Jesus stated that "the meek shall inherit the earth" (Mt 5:5) in His Sermon on the Mount, He meant those who develop disciplined power, disciplined personalities, will end up inheriting the earth. It was a term commonly used 2000 years ago to describe and even complement chariot war horses of the Roman Empire. It is usually preferable and certainly more noble to be a chariot war horse than a donkey.

From China approximately 2,500 years ago, Lao Tzu echos

this wisdom in #33 of the Tao Te Ching: "Knowing others is wisdom; Knowing the self is enlightenment. Mastering others requires force; Mastering the self needs strength. To die but not to perish is to be eternally present."

PRAYER IS ESSENTIAL

WISDOM

The older I get,

the more gray I see.

Yet the things of the light sharpen

as life's shadows extend and deepen.

Chapter 15
Prayers For Jack

In the winter of 1971 - 72 the older brother of the girl across the street from me in the small subdivision where we lived, was diagnosed with a brain tumor. The girl, Debbie, was one of two girls who instigated and promoted hatred and lies about me, my sister, and the rest of my family when we first moved to Illinois. Within weeks of moving into our new home, most of the kids from our small subdivision of eight or nine families were aligned with Debbie and Kathy against me, my sister, and my brother for no good reason at all. It was completely irrational and unwarranted; an intense adolescent hazing. Looking back, it seems that we were unwitting lightening rods for their own problems. There was no way to avoid them easily, especially because my sister and I rode the school bus with them. My brother was still in elementary school which meant he took a different school bus.

What made it worse was that soon other kids from other bus stops were picking on us too. Interestingly, every kid who picked on us came from a sick home, just we as did. "Dysfunctional" sounds too sanitized to express all of the pathology, violence, mental and spiritual sickness, alcoholism, adultery, incest, or whatever else that takes place in too many homes year after year. Nearly every family is somewhat dysfunctional to varying degrees. For many families the word "dysfunctional" is too mild; "screwed-up" is more appropriate. Us kids on the bus kind of fell into three classic roles for people who are abused. Some were abusers, others the victims, while a smaller group was a mix of both. These roles often carry over into adulthood, generally more subtle and insidious.

I remember Jack, Debbie's older brother, as being very mean and aggressive, filled with anger, even hatred. If there was one person I feared more than anybody else during that period in my life, it was Jack. There were bullies on my street in Ohio but I could usually avoid them. Similarly in California, I could usually avoid the bad guys out there. But this was different. The guy lived right across the street from me and right next door to my only friend in the neighborhood. There was no easy, convenient way to avoid him. For the first couple of years that we lived in Lake Barrington, he made my life very difficult, adding to the struggles I already had to deal with. There were many times when he would see me from a distance and would come charging after me. Because he was older and bigger (he was in high school and I was in junior high) and because I lacked self-confidence and upper body strength, I would do my best to avoid him. To visit my friend Ron who lived next to Jack and Debbie's family home, I often had to walk within several feet of him.

I have never understood why he hated me. I can imagine that he was mad at me because I rejected Debbie's wish that I be her boyfriend. I was foolish enough to tell her that I liked her friend, Terri. How could I know that she would take the news like a psycho? Maybe I led her on a little but not more than a week or two. And its not like we had kids and a mortgage together. We just talked and played kick-the-can with other kids (similar to hide-and-go-seek). Unfortunately, as usually happens with a target person or group, other reasons to hate me and harass me were added on to my original sin of not liking his sister. Being a wise guy did not help my cause either. With his irrational and over-the-top anger, Jack found plenty of reasons to hate me and to attack me.

When I learned that he had a malignant brain tumor, I was happy. Nobody was very hopeful that he would live. Finally! Someone (of the many) who had attacked and abused me for just being alive was getting what they deserved. I had come to hate Jack. In retrospect, I think that I focused a lot of my anger, pain, and frustration onto him. I was glad to learn that one of the bad guys in my life was going to "get it".

Fortunately, sometime in probably February, 1972 I had the

bright idea of praying for my enemy. I credit the Holy Spirit for planting this thought in my head, for reminding me of scriptures I had heard and learned in church. There are several verses throughout the Old and New Testaments that teach the practice of love and kindness to enemies. However, Luke 6:27 - 38 and Romans 12:14, 19-21 state most closely what I was thinking. If I prayed for Jack in an honest, loving way I thought that I would be making him suffer, to "heap the burning coals on his head". In other words, I thought that I could get in some payback to him for bullying me. So I began praying for him and to a lesser extent, his family too, at least once every day for the next three to four months. I asked God to remind me everyday until it became a habit. God did and it became a habit for me to always pray for Jack.

Shortly after I began praying for him, I had no doubt that God would heal him, that he would not die. True enough, he did not die. I know that my prayers, along with everyone else's prayers and the medical treatment, helped him survive. He healed and lived for another 15+ years or so. Sadly, I recently learned that he did die later as the cancer returned.

What I did not realize when I began praying for Jack was that I would be blessed greatly by God for denying myself, my natural human desire for vengeance, instead practicing love toward an "enemy". Sometimes I think that I got more out that habit of prayer for Jack than Jack did. Indeed, Jesus taught, *"But love your enemies; do good to them and lend to them without expecting to get anything back. Then your reward will be great; and you will be sons of the Most High, because He is kind to the ungrateful and wicked. Be merciful, just as your Father is merciful."* Luke 6:35-36. By praying for Jack with a soft heart, I became healed of my hatred for him.

At first it was very difficult to let go of my pain and anger, but it became much easier with daily practice and with help from God. I believe that this specific episode helped develop my ability to pray for people who persecute or attack me; to forgive others who hurt or anger me. Also, this blessed ability to let go of pain and anger is what helped save me later and ultimately helped me heal from my own sick family life. Unlike love, with which you can be drunk, hatred makes you wired. Wired with anger. It is not intoxicating, but it is addictive. It preoccupies your mind and your energy. Like weapons-grade radioactive material, hatred is toxic to the possessor as well as the subject of the hatred.

Although Jack and I never became friends, there seemed to be a softening of his attitude toward me. His anger seemed to leave him. During and especially after the specific crisis of Jack being very ill, he became humbled, wounded, more gentle. Also, his family, including Debbie, seemed to change, with their family anger lessening. Perhaps my prayers for Jack and his family contributed in some way helping them transform their troubled interpersonal dynamics or at least their relationship toward me. In any case, I am very glad that I did pray for Jack. Over the years, praying for my "enemies" or difficult people has become an important and good habit. Sometimes I have even made new friends. It is always amazing when people, including myself, change due to the miraculous mystery of prayer.

Chapter 16

Presence

Sometime in late 1974 or early 1975 I purchased a small pamphlet on Brother Lawrence from my church's bookstore. After doing other things with his life, he became a Discalced Carmelite lay brother (a monk). He lived in Paris and worked as a cook for the order for 30 years. He lived to the age of 80 years old (b. 1611; d. 1691). He never specifically wrote much about his spiritual life and insights save for what is shared in a few letters to friends and in some simple spiritual notes.

He developed a deep, rich spirituality primarily through training his mind, his heart, his being to always be aware of the presence of God no matter what he was doing. Thus, while he was busy peeling potatoes or otherwise serving his Carmelite brothers, he was in conscious, prayerful dialog or rest with God. It was in his daily work in the kitchen and not in the chapel or on some "mountaintop" that he cultivated a deep friendship with God. He was in the world but not distracted by it to the degree of postponing or neglecting that most important primary relationship with God. I was very impressed by this when I read it.

It seemed very novel yet sublime to practice being aware of the presence of God. How very radical! God is ever-present anyway, and once the filter of space-time is removed from the lens of our consciousness, presumably we will live and exist in a far more direct (less filtered) revelation and experience of God. Thus, I reasoned, why not start now with getting to know God and to live in awareness of His presence as much as humanly possible? To accept the awareness of His presence is a fundamental aspect of expanding human consciousness: to become continually aware of God and to gracefully live within that daily experience; to transcend our natural self-preoccupation to live in an ever-expanding life. The question that begs to be asked is to

Whom or What does our consciousness aspire? What is our most common default mode for our minds and hearts? To where, what, or who do our minds and emotions drift to rest when we are not actively thinking or feeling? These types of thoughts began to bounce through the hallways of my mind, knocking things over, zigzagging in various directions.

One morning, shortly after waking up, I decided that I would spend every possible moment of that day telling God that I loved Him — just to see what would happen. As I drove to school, attended my high school classes, and ate lunch, I constantly repeated a couple very simple prayers to God telling Him that I loved Him. If I got distracted or needed to pay attention to something in a class, as soon as I remembered, I brought my mind back to praising God, speaking directly to Him. Soon I was experiencing a very deep peace that passed all understanding. I continued with my prayers. And then it happened.

While driving home from school in the early afternoon I had a gentle, overpowering explosion of bliss. It was way beyond joy. I felt it well-up inside of me then percolate in bubbles or waves of ecstasy. It was amazing. The percolating ecstasy lasted only a few moments but the resulting bliss pervaded my being for the rest of the afternoon. I had been taken or graced to a new level of intimacy with the Holy Spirit.

When I got home 20 minutes or so after the moment of ecstasy, my mother was very angry. She accused me of being high on drugs. This was despite my explanations to the contrary and despite my perfectly clear, normal eyes. For quite awhile her anger and haranguing could not touch me. I was way beyond her. But slowly she began to erode the deep, deep peace that I had. I didn't want to be around her — she was literally bringing me down. I had to get away. I had to be alone. Finally, after several minutes, I was able to slip off to my room to enjoy my gift from God and to reflect on it. In retrospect, my experience is reminiscent of Jesus' disciples on the day of Pentecost, as recorded in the opening chapters of the Book of Acts in the New

Testament. Their fellow citizens in Jerusalem accused them of being drunk on wine when actually they were suddenly and powerfully filled with the Holy Spirit.

About ten years later, in complement to this experience, I had a powerful revelation regarding the presence of God. In the Fall of 1985 I was living and working in the Seattle area as an outside salesman. I was busy learning how to sell dictation equipment to "make my monthly quota". My initial sales territory included southern King County and most of the Olympic Peninsula. It was a perfect detox from the flat, boring urban landscape of the Chicago area. My territory was huge and spread out. I often spent as much or more time driving to sales appointments as I did cold calling or meeting with customers. The driving allowed me to contemplate various topics and questions. It also allowed God to zap me with insights and ideas, revelations and connections.

The revelation I had regarding the presence of God was this: it dawned on me that the most powerful and profound gift anyone could ever have is the gift of the awareness of God's presence. (The gift of life is implied by this because to be aware of God implies that the being is alive.) Initially, as you struggle to cultivate the habit of always being aware of God, it may feel as effort-full as when you stare at one of those recently popular 3D design patterns. However, with persistence, your point of focus shifts and a three dimensional scene emerges that was invisible a moment earlier. Even when your eyes shift in focus back to the original picture pattern only, the picture will never be the same again. You know and have experienced a dynamic dimension that exists within yet is transcendent of the easily visible. So it is with awareness of the Divine. Being aware of God causes a field shift of your mind and heart. Divine awareness alters thoughts and emotions. It alters our speech and our actions. In short, it reorders our being much as a magnet held underneath a piece of cardboard alters and reorders iron filings on the topside of the cardboard.

Awareness of God certainly has changed me and countless

others through the years in every culture and society humanity has ever created. And that change in me and in others has been for the better. We are all better than we were before. Even in my prodigal days I was aware of God. It helped me understand which direction my true home was regardless if I was in the swamp of sin, or the desert of emptiness, or caught in a storm of confusion. Awareness is the beginning of intimate experience of and with God. It is the omnidirectional signal in any reality that comforts and guides all beings that desire to be comforted and guided. I wonder why I for so long resisted or even denied the seductive call, the ultimate longing in my heart?

Chapter 17
Changing Paths

A topic that has long fascinated me is the calculus of divine guidance. The question of whether there is a Supreme Being that possesses self-awareness, self-will, morality, is involved with the created order, and is not limited except in respect to the free will of creatures that have the capacity for it has been moot for me since I was a young child. However, the question that immediately follows will never be satisfactorily answered. How does God lead, guide, and remain involved in my life and in the lives of others? Related questions include how can two people, both of whom claim to love and follow God, end up with opposing understandings of what they think is God's will for their individual or shared situations?

Obvious answers include His revelations as recorded in the Bible; belonging to a faith community (i.e. a Christian church); the good counsel of others; science; and simply using our God-given intelligence to assess and make proper or good decisions. These are all adequate and useful answers. But these answers fail to penetrate the actual mystery of Divine guidance. That is, how does God actually lead and guide people, including those who do not have a relationship with Him, in their everyday actions, specifically without violating our free will such that His "will be done on earth as it is in heaven"?

Humans tend to naturally perceive and interact with reality in a logical, sequential, mechanical manner, perceiving cause and effect involving one or perhaps two variables at the most. We live our lives within the mechanics of a Newtonian world, unaware of the Einsteinian quantum universe all around us that permeates everything that exists. Our awareness, our understanding of what is or should be normal is similar to the simplicity of arithmetic: everything adds up but there is so much more.

In contrast, the Supreme Being, God the Father, is able to keep track of an apparently infinite number of variables and vectors that weave together into an intelligible universe and meaningful lives. This is divine multi-variate calculus (with chaos, fractals, and strings, too).

An example of how infinitely limited our human minds are is the game of trying to keep track of several traffic lights along one long main street, each with different light cycles triggered by slightly different events, while at the same time visualizing all of the cars and pedestrians on each cross street and the speed and direction in which they all are moving in relation to the main street. Now imagine all of the different conversations or thoughts each person is having and all of the different things that each person might be seeing. Add to this, all of the different reasons for each person to be moving in and out of the area of the main street. Yet you are still far from the full or complete perception of the defined area of the main street with it's cross streets. It is very difficult to conceptualize, if not impossible. This is just one small section of the world and an even smaller, nearly inconsequential speck of the entire known universe. Furthermore, it focuses only on what is conceivable as the "present". Yet God the Father is able to track and know all of these variables and vectors such that meaning and intelligibility are created and sustained both in the present and for all times to come.

To deny that there is a God who can create and know and be involved with all these things is similar to clay questioning the potter regarding what he is making. (Isaiah 45: 9 in the Old Testament or Romans 11: 33-36 in the New testament.) Who wants a god that a human mind can fully know?

Personally, I really enjoyed living in Seattle. Yet a gradual dissatisfaction, a creeping emptiness of meaning seeped into my life creating a damp despair. As unwelcome as it first was, I gradually came to accept that I needed to make a change in order to restore my life to full meaning. A few people had suggested that I attend law school. This appealed to me as I was tired of outside sales. Once I began to prayerfully consider my situation, I knew that in order to continue growing, to continue being my authentic self rather than clinging to who I was or might have wanted to be, I needed to go to graduate school. Continuing prayer confirmed this, deepening into a conviction. While sad to leave my life at the time as well as to leave Seattle, I was also energized by the new adventure.

I did decide to attend law school. I also wanted to earn an MBA. With both degrees, I figured I would be "bullet proof" in the business world. I decided to move to Lincoln, Nebraska to attend UNL. My brother was enrolled there, finishing a Masters degree in Remote Sensing and Computer Programming. Thus I would not be alone, I would be living with one of my best friends at the time. In Lincoln I spent two months of daily searching for steady, decent employment necessary for the upcoming year that I needed to prepare for grad school. However, nothing worked out. Although it had been an important time for my brother and I to be together, I knew that I had to move somewhere else in order to find a job that would support my life.

I prayed about returning to the Chicago area. I drove off to a lonely place outside the city of Lincoln. It seemed to make sense both logically and prayerfully. The gentle interior resistance or pressure of the Holy Spirit's "hand" was not opposed to my moving back to Chicago. I began packing later that day as I did not have much remaining money I had earned from the various temp jobs I worked in Lincoln.

When contemplating the calculus of divine guidance we must understand that we, as humans, only exist in context. We do not exist independently of any or all other things. That is, we exist only in realm of creation. The ultimate, both beginning and final, context in which we exist is in relationship to our Creator, who dwells beyond all things but participates within His universe of created universes. This is absolute irregardless of whether we acknowledge this fact or not. Our perception or assent does not alter this fact of existence just as ignoring gravity does make it go away or cause it to cease affecting our daily lives. He is the omnidirectional center of all things, yet beyond all things simultaneously.

Our lives are linked to many other lives, of people known and unknown to us. Our prayers and His guidance incorporates consideration of all others who are or may be linked to each one of us and our lives. Thus I knew that if He was guiding me or at least approving of me returning to Chicago, there would be a job waiting for me someway, somehow. It would be up to me to find it, which is as it should be because only I can live my life.

I arrived at my mother's house early Easter morning in April 1987. It is a nine hour drive from Lincoln to Fox River Grove, a northwest suburb of Chicago. The next day I made a couple of telephone calls. By dinner time Monday night I had a full-time job in commodities again earning a salary that paid more than what I had been earning in sales in Washington.

Nine months later, the firm I was working for was purchased by a British trading company. Some positions were eliminated. .My supervisor had felt uncomfortable with me for the time I worked there because somehow I threatened him both as a person and somehow as a Christian. Sometimes you do not need to say anything for the Holy Spirit within you to convict others who reject God. I did not lose that job because I was incompetent or unruly.

I had relied on God for the past nine months, praying throughout each work day. That day was no different. I knew what my supervisor, Roger, was planning and I prayed to God about it, knowing — trusting — that He had already known or anticipated my situation. I confidently asked God for help and for His peace. Rather than speak directly with me, Roger asked one of my coworkers to tell me that I was fired. Steve asked me to go with him downstairs to a lounge on the first floor of the Chicago Board of Trade. He was nervous while I was relaxed, trusting that my God, the Sovereign Creator of all universes, was going to take care of me just as He had a hundred times before.

146

Steve ordered a drink, offering to buy me one. I declined because I wanted to stay straight. I wanted to be ready to interview for the next job I hoped would be available later that day somewhere with someone else. After our meeting in which Steve told me I was fired, I called a friend named Lonny. He told me of a career position that had just opened up at another trading firm. The local supervisor there had an immediate need for a balancer and outtrade clerk. I was qualified for both as I had been doing that work for the preceding nine months. I called and scheduled an interview for later that day.

When I took the train home that night, I had a new job at a higher salary. I praised God a lot. He had again provided for my needs. It seems that because I tried to act with honor as a person of faith, God treated me with honor, even protected me. As Paul once wrote in his letter to new believers who lived in Rome, "And we know that in all things God works for the good of those who love him.....If God is for us, who can be against us?" Romans 8: 28-31. Divine guidance and protection in this difficult world, experienced through a simple trust, is a wonderful way to live life and to interact with others.

Chapter 18

An Answer to Prayer

Seeing her sitting there on the couch made me curious. "Who is she?" I wondered to myself.

By the second or third time of seeing her sitting on the lounge couch just outside my dormitory section, I inexplicably knew that I could have a deep relationship with her. This made me even more curious about her. That the Holy Spirit could finally be showing me a woman who would quell my lifelong desire for a soulmate filled me with both wonder and caution. Why now? Why after all this time and adventure? On the other hand, why not?

I sensed that she was not from the United States, although she did not look foreign. From experience I knew that the best way to meet a woman from another culture is to be introduced by mutual acquaintances instead of the American way of just walking up to her without an introduction. Thus, I had to wait a couple of weeks for the proper opportunity to meet her. My patience paid off one evening in the dormitory cafeteria. The mystery woman was having dinner with a couple of guys who lived on my dorm floor. They were architectural graduate students, so I guessed that maybe she was one too. Acting quickly, I asked Diego or Mark to introduce me to her. Within a moment, I finally met Doris. We sat together, eating dinner with our mutual acquaintances.

I found her to be very attractive in every manner of the word. She was from Puerto Rico, liked art and poetry, and was at IIT to earn a Masters degree in Architecture. I liked her dark hair and eyes as well as her easy-going laugh. She had a good sense of humor. She possessed a dignity and poise uncommon to many people in my society. Best of all, she seemed to like me. I mean, at least she didn't run in the other direction whenever she saw me after that first dinner in the cafeteria. After a few more meals together in the neutrality of the cafeteria, I wrote her a note asking her out to dinner. I slipped it under her dorm room door.

She was hesitant, not really certain about going on a date with a gringo. Fortunately, she found the courage to accept my invitation. Within a day or two Doris called me to accept and to learn what time to be ready that coming Saturday. Although I was tremendously preoccupied with my first semester in law school, the remainder of the week was spiced with the sweet anticipation of taking Doris out to dinner.

Our dinner date was perfect. It was so perfect that she did not return my calls and avoided me for a few days afterward. I was stunned more than disappointed. I couldn't believe it! I had met this wonderful woman with whom I had a great chemistry, we had a date that suspended time, and now she was not communicating with me. I was beginning to wonder if God was playing a dirty trick on me. After about a week, Doris called me. She apologized for avoiding me and asked me to visit her to talk. "I'm sorry" are two very rare words these days. Impressed by her apology, I immediately went to her dorm to talk with her. Our friendship and love quickly grew from that moment onward.

The only reason I was at IIT/Chicago-Kent was because when I returned to Chicago from Seattle I resumed working in the commodities industry. In the "holding pattern" while preparing to apply to and attend a law school somewhere, I became acquainted with one of the trading firm's attorneys who had attended Chicago-Kent. I only applied to two different law schools, really only wanting to go to Chicago-Kent. It is amazing how ethereal, tenuous, and mundane Divine Guidance so often appears to be. However, all things do seem work together for the good of those who love God. We married in August 1989, twelve months after we first met. We have been together ever since.

It has been said that marriage is the crucible for the human spirit. Great growth and refinement can be achieved through this fundamental and dynamic human relationship. This has been the case with us. We have struggled greatly for years because of finances, our families, and the effort it takes to establish a good career in contemporary US society. Most importantly, we have struggled greatly because of the need to heal and mature in freedom from negative patterns of interacting inherited from others. Specific techniques and skills learned in marriage counseling from a skilled therapist named Pat continue to be helpful in how we share feelings and prompted us to adopt good rules for healthy disagreements. Pat also pointed out to us certain codependencies acquired earlier in our lives that were interfering with our marriage and needed to be shed. We worked hard to free ourselves from those codependencies. Because of our collaborative labor of love, we have grown and healed tremendously over the past thirteen years. Our marriage and the friendship upon which it is based have deepened and strengthened over the years. It keeps getting better and better.

Because Doris and I have tried to keep God and the teachings of Christ present in our marriage, we have learned to give each other the benefit of the doubt during times of disagreement or simple miscommunication. I easily forgive Doris for real or perceived wrongs. Although I still struggle at times, I have grown in my ability to listen to her regarding changes I can make to eliminate points of conflict or simply to accommodate her preference in certain matters. We are able to do this because we both believe and trust that God is the third person in our relationship. He lives in both our hearts and helps provide objectivity, the ability to see beyond our individual positions. We try to be sensitive to His guidance. This has helped me to remain open and trusting with Doris. In turn, the tempering and changes we have experienced in our marriage have helped us become more patient, objective, and empathetic with the rest of the world, too.

However, despite our best hopes and efforts, by Summer 1997 we seriously questioned if we should remain married. The years of struggle, our different careers, and divergent interests were tearing at our bond, our mutual commitment to each other. At past crisis points, we turned to God in prayer, both together and separately. This crisis period, however, was different. We were tired of the struggle to achieve harmony in our friendship. Like people swimming against a riptide, we were exhausted and ready to give up. Yet, no matter how disgusted I was with the situation, or how tired I was of her anger toward our life that was often directed at me, the Holy Spirit would urge me to try again, not to give up. I would fantasize about being free from her and our marriage. But it would begin to hurt too much. I had to stay married to her although things seemed too far gone. I did not really know what was going on with her although the Holy Spirit continued to give me insight into her thoughts and feelings. Things were bad. We were both angry that unrelenting struggle in our lives, most of it external to us, was about to be victorious over us.

It was then that I rediscovered fasting. I had not fasted for many years, since I stopped trying to force myself into holiness twenty years earlier. I cannot tell you exactly why (no one can) sincere fasting might move God or help in a struggle but I decided to try it again. For several weeks during Autumn 1997 I fasted and prayed once each week. I told no one. It was just between God and me. I prayed earnestly for healing and a turnaround in our marriage. I prayed for a renewed and abundant love for Doris. I prayed to make changes in myself that were contributing to marital friction. Mostly I prayed for God's help and for His will to be done, not mine, not Doris', not evil's. This crisis was a critical catharsis of a few months that helped our marriage grow deeper, healthier, and more authentic than ever before. Wonderfully, it continues to trend that way.

Renewed mutual commitment, additional unlearning of corrosive habits of interacting, a lot of painful but gentle honesty, and the difficult work of personal change have been essential to our healing as a couple. Overall, our continuing strategic advantage is our mutual friendship with the living Christ.

Acknowledging God to be in the center of our relationship, coupled with prayer and even fasting as needed, strongly tipped the odds in our favor of staying married and for renewing our friendship.

The other thing that really helped me trust the situation and weather the crisis is that I don't believe He brings couples together planning to have them divorce later. I remain convinced that He brought us together in the first place, believing in us. Consequently, I am encouraged because if He knows it to be possible, then I should believe it too. My trust in Him inspires me to give my very best until such time it becomes clear that my marriage with Doris and God has died or changed in some irrevocable way such that divorce becomes the healthier path.

One of the greatest gifts or fruits of our marriage is our son It began the moment Doris and I first suspected she was pregnant. I raced out and bought two home pregnancy test kits from two different manufacturers as a check against a false positive. Both test strips immediately indicated new life inside her. It was at once frightening and exhilarating for us. My life forever changed for the better in that moment.

My daily privilege and responsibility since that moment nearly nine years ago is to be present and attentive as a good father for my son. It is one of the most important things I will ever do. I love being his father. For me, it began the moment I learned Doris was pregnant. At least once every day during her pregnancy and every night during his first year of life, I put my hand over our son and prayed for him, thanking God for him. I prayed, and still do though not necessarily every single day, that the Holy Spirit will be with him all the days of his life, that God will continue to form good character in him, and that he will always be protected. He is a fine person with a good heart and a clear mind. I think but am not certain, again at the juncture of belief and knowing, that my prayers for him have somehow, mysteriously contributed to who he is and is becoming. I have wondered more than once what might happen if parents all around the world began praying every day for their children beginning when they are in the womb, asking God to bless them with good hearts and minds, strong character and deep faith. It would be a revolution, a true evolution or step forward for humanity.

To my happy discovery, my relationship with my son has greatly and deeply healed me from the earlier traumas in my life. The things I missed in my relationship with my father and family I now experience with my son in a healthy manner. I love being his parent and friend. It doesn't really matter anymore that I did not get in my youth what every child deserves. Being in relationship with my son healed those wounds in my personality. One of the things I enjoy sharing with him is my faith. The seeds of faith are already growing deep and strong in him. In time, he will have the opportunity and challenge, if he so decides, of making it truly his own. I hope that his faith will serve him as well as mine has me.

The reason why I am a good father is due to my relationship with Jesus Christ. He has been the greatest positive influence on me. I have learned from Him, from how He loves and treats me, of how I should treat others especially those over whom I have power and authority. His Spirit guides and inspires me to be gentle, patient, and kind with my son. It isn't always easy and I sometimes fall short of what he needs. But then I either realize I was wrong or my wife points it out to me. I apologize to him, and we go on from there. Together, my son, wife, and I contribute to our family life from which we draw strength and joy.

Truly, God does answer prayers, though it requires patient trust in Him. I would not be as healthy, happy, and centered as I am but for my wife's love, friendship, and challenges to heal, grow, serve, and enjoy. "A wife of noble character who can find? She is worth more than rubies. Her husband has full confidence in her and lacks nothing of value. She brings him good, not harm, all the days of her life." Proverbs 31: 10-12.

KNOWING GOD & SELF
MORE DEEPLY
AND
CLEARLY

Smasher of idols,
      destroyer of truths.
            Divine.

Cleanser of decay,
      giver of new life.
            Divine.

Breath and being can now
become prayer.

Divine presence provides
presents of the Divine.

Awareness of Divine invites
and develops Divine awareness.

Chapter 19

An Act of Mercy; An Act of Sin

In January or February 1979, in the spirit of rebellion, I ingested a psychedelic drug while partying with my brother and some of his friends. I did this with sadness in my heart and over the protests of the Holy Spirit. But I wanted to do it, in large part because I was still mad at God for having allowed that spirit guide to mess with me (Hydroplaning). I wanted to hurt His feelings. Sometimes, "when you got to sin, you got to sin." Several hours later, I was laying on my bed trying to settle down and sleep. I was still buzzing on the pot, beer, and the psychedelic powder one of my brother's friends had nicknamed, "Crank" because it made you wired, among other effects.

I specifically asked Jesus to help me. I apologized for interrupting my friendship with Him by taking the drugs and getting buzzed on alcohol. I had purposely drank enough beer to make it easier for me to ignore the Holy Spirit, which made it easier for me to take the drugs. I promised to never take drugs again. A moment after praying, the drug effect quickly and suddenly toned down, almost completely removed from me, which allowed me to sleep. Although this episode was not as bothersome and frightening as my experience on Columbus Day 1975, the drug effects were annoying me, creating a deepening distress. I was grateful that Jesus forgave me and was kind to me.

A couple weeks later I smoked pot again. It was a character flaw of mine mixed with continuing flare-ups of anger and rebellion at God or at my life. I had to struggle to ignore the Holy Spirit's vigorous protests to not do it. The entire time I was high I clearly felt His disapproval, as I always did whenever I got high after I made the deeper surrender to God in August 1977 (Season of Emptiness / Sea Change).

I really do not have a good excuse for getting high occasion-

157

ally during those first couple of years of my new life. In part, I would get high due to lack of personal discipline and lack of respect for myself. I had deeply ingrained self-defeating behavior acquired during the first several years of my life due to the abuse I had suffered. I had learned to abuse myself. The other key reason why I got high was because I was selfish to the point of disobedience to the guidance and desires of the Holy Spirit. Being very sensitive to God initially often felt like I was sharing a small 5' x 7' tent with a large, 7'10" basketball player. My consciousness often felt crowded or cramped. I could not move or sit or lie down or look anywhere within the scope of my consciousness and not "see" or interact with God. It used to be very disconcerting to have such a strong sense of God's presence. It was almost overwhelming at times. I felt that the only way for me to get some "breathing room" was to temporarily break fellowship with the Holy Spirit through occasional, deliberate acts of disobedience. My weakness for getting high on occasion was for a few years my "thorn in the flesh". Fortunately over the past 24+ years we have learned to live gracefully with each other within me and within my life. With God's help and my hard work, I have overcome my self-destructive behaviors and thoughts. I have decreased and He has increased, yet in a wonderful paradox, I am more myself today than I was yesterday. Increasingly, there is more room in the tent of my being for the both of us. I no longer feel like Hosea's unfaithful wife. (Refer to the Old Testament book of the same name).

The reasons that I believe that God does not want me getting high using drugs are: (1) To not open myself to STDs - spiritually transmitted disease or contamination by evil; (2) To not disrupt fellowship with Him. It is like coming home drunk to your wife — it is not appreciated; it is destructive to the relationship; (3) His desire for me to live a healthy and productive life, not one dissipated through drugs or too much alcohol; (4) To be a valid witness to others concerning His desire and transformative love to redeem and sanctify His creation, beginning with humanity;

and (5) Nowadays, there is too much blood associated with the use of drugs. The selfishness required to take drugs is at the expense of other people's deaths in producing and marketing the drugs. People from families to entire countries suffer due to the illicit drug trade. Entire societies, most notably Columbia, are in serious danger of violent subversion due to the international drug trade. I have absolutely no right to help harm or destroy other people, their societies, and the environment just so I can have my happy little high. Please clearly note that He has never guided me away from having fun and enjoying various things. I still drink beer, play catch, and so forth. He simply does not want me sinning, which is falling short of who I can be. The greatest thing I can ever do is to be myself in Christ, that is, in friendship with God. Furthermore, if God is the source of all life, it makes sense to pursue that relationship first and foremost, no matter the passing cost. Drugs, like any other sin, are destructive personally and corporately.

So there I was, laying in bed enjoying my marihuana high. Suddenly, I felt an unseen finger pressing hard on my sternum. Words formed in my mind, felt more than heard or thought.

"What about your promise to Me?"

"What promise?" I replied, knowing exactly what He meant.

"Your promise to not use drugs again."

"Oh that. I made that promise while I was high and upset. It is not a valid promise."

I was arguing the legal principle that contracts or agreements made under duress are typically not binding or valid.

"Leave me alone," I continued. "I'm high, I sinned. It's unfair for You to hold me to that promise. I was desperate when I made it."

I strongly felt Jesus' anger, hurt, disappointment, and frustration.

A couple days later, missing His presence and feeling repentant, I asked Him to forgive me. Although I believe that I received it immediately, it took a couple of hours after that before I felt Him close to me again. I had strained our friendship and intimacy. I had been a jerk to God. Fortunately He forgave me. He "turned the other cheek". Through situations such as this one, I have learned that His friendship is not cheap, not something to be abused or manipulated. He is not someone I can take for granted, available at my beck and call. But He is present for all who sincerely want forgiveness and who at least try to change. He may fill our nets with fish, but first we have to throw the nets, usually many times. (John 21: 1-14).

Chapter 20

The Divine Iconoclast

During Christmas Break 1979-80, after praying about it, I knew that I needed to further distance myself from both my parents and their ongoing bitter feud. I was tired of being put in the middle or being manipulated by either side. Cutting off from my father's monetary support was an important act of distancing. However, because I did not have any savings at the time, I knew that this act of freedom and health meant that I would need to withdraw from Oregon State University for a while. Fortunately, if I became a resident of Oregon by residing in the state for twelve months without being enrolled in any college level courses, tuition would drop 66%, making it easier for me to support myself and pay for my education.

Upon returning to Oregon in early January, I began looking for a job. Unfortunately my prospects of securing a job, any job, were not good. In 1980 the US was in the midst of a severe economic recession. In any recession, housing starts tend to drop off quickly and sharply. In 1980 Oregon's economy was, and still is to an extent, heavily dependent upon logging and related lumber activities tied into housing starts. In Benton County where I lived, the unemployment rate was nearly 25%. I had my January rent covered which gave me slightly less than 31 days to secure a new place to live and to find a job. Importantly, I trusted God because if He was leading me to put greater distance between myself and my parents, He had already made provisions for my needs, some way, somehow. It was up to me to figure it out as I walked by faith each day, like a game of discovery. Although concerned, I was not too worried. I knew that He would take care of me.

It was at this time that I had a dream. In the very conscious dream, I was in love with a beautiful woman. I asked her to marry me. She turned around, walked past several interested men who seemed to be other suitors, and approached her father. She asked him for permission to marry me. He said yes. In the next scene in my dream we turned and walked away from an alter together, just married. Much joy and blessings showered upon us. When the beautiful mystery woman had turned around to ask her father for permission to marry me, I noticed that her jet black hair was in a pony tail pinned back up onto her head. I thought right there in the dream that it was odd that she had to ask her father for permission to marry me. Afterall, this is America at the end of the 20th century. Although a man may ask his fiancé's parents for permission to marry their daughter, I had never ever heard of anyone asking their own parents for permission to marry. The dream ended as suddenly as it had begun. I returned to the "regularly scheduled" dreaming. When I awoke the next morning, all I could think of was that dream. It was the kind of dream that is so tangible your heart is stirred with hope, causing you to wonder for a day or two afterward if it will come true. Though the dream slowly lost its intensity or immediacy, it lingered like a sweet fragrance of hope in my heart's memory.

During January and February 1980 I stayed in touch with the campus Global Studies Office. During Fall Term 1979 I had been a volunteer Program Coordinator. As such, I had the rare privilege of meeting and hosting or assisting various authors, economists, UN personnel, policy advisors, and so forth. I was able to discuss all sorts of topics and insights with them on a one-to-one basis. It was fun and fascinating. I learned a lot. Just because I was not currently enrolled at OSU did not mean that I could not still assist the Director in his various duties.

One day in late January I popped into the office to see what was going on. Another, new, student volunteer named Janet was there. As we chatted, I asked both her and Eric, the Director of the Global Studies Office, if either one of them knew of any work available. I must have also mentioned that as of February 1st I would have no place to live.

"You know, I gave a ride to a hitchhiker the other day," Janet said. "He is a volunteer fireman with the Philomath Fire Department. He said that they are taking applications for one or two sleepers."

Philomath is a small logging town of about 1000 people situated on the eastern edge of the Coast Range, only 5 or 6 miles west of Corvallis.

"What's a sleeper?" I asked.

"I don't really know, but I think that a "sleeper" is a volunteer fireman who lives at the station for free in exchange for being on call for fires or medical emergencies."

"Hey. Thanks. I'm going to check it out. I was just getting ready to live in the Coast Range or something. Thanks!" I was excited.

I went to the Philomath Fire Department within the next day or two and completed an application. The Department would review all of the applications at their next monthly meeting which was scheduled for (if I remember correctly) the second Tuesday of February, just as every monthly meeting is always the second Tuesday of each month.

I went back to the Global Studies Office later that week to thank Janet again for the housing tip. While there, Eric tossed a couple of tickets for a Persian dinner and Bahai presentation to me.

"I can't go to it. I have a schedule conflict. You can go," he said.

"Wow! Thanks! I had wanted to go but did not buy a ticket because I am almost out of money. I want to learn more about the Bahai faith or religion," I said. The dinner was scheduled for the next evening on campus.

I attended the event, sitting with a couple of people that I knew from classes on campus. The food was delicious and the speech on the Bahai faith was interesting. After the program I went to the literature tables that were set-up in the rear of the auditorium. It was at the literature tables that I saw her for the first time. She was a beautiful Persian woman who was a graduate student at OSU. I was asking and discussing many questions regarding the Bahai religion with a guy who was about the same age as myself. His name was Bruce.

At one point the beautiful Persian woman must have overheard me talking with Bruce about the Bahai faith and it's relationship to other religions such as Christianity and Islam. She introduced herself and, along with Bruce, invited me to a party that some members of the local Bahai community were hosting later that week on Saturday night.

"You should come to a party we are going to Saturday night. You can learn more about the Bahai faith," Vashti said.

"OK. Thanks! I can probably go. I want to learn more about your faith and how it relates to the other religions," I said. I also wanted to learn more about Vashti. I was intrigued by her.

The following Saturday evening, I showered and dressed for the party. I wouldn't know anyone except for my two new acquaintances from the dinner presentation earlier that week. Naturally, I was a little nervous about going to the party. I hesitated at the last minute even though I was ready to go. I knew that there would not be any alcohol there. I was not certain that I wanted to go to a house full of strangers without a glass of beer or wine to take the edge off my shyness in meeting new people. In my mind, I wavered back and forth. By the time I decided to flip a coin to force the decision, the party had already begun. Two out of three: heads I go, tails I stay. Sometimes fate is only a coin toss away from happening. I flipped the quarter. First toss: heads. Second toss: tails. Third toss: heads. I had to go to the party. It took a moment for me to accept the coin toss results but then I dutifully went.

When I arrived, Bruce and two or three other people I recognized from the dinner presentation were gathered in or on the edge of the kitchen, with other party-goers scattered throughout the first floor of the house. Vashti was present too, but I played it cool. I figured that she probably attracted a lot of attention from men, so I consciously sought to distinguish myself.

As with so many other areas in life, when it comes to beautiful women, you are either a groupie, a predator, or a peer. For quality relationships, only a peer relationship will work. However, this is easier said than done when you are in the middle of an extended drought and you suddenly stumble upon a cool, refreshing spring. The thirst for love and a relationship can be so overpowering that you throw yourself into the waters of love, impatient to quench your thirst, your pain. But in so doing, dirt and sand are often kicked into the very water you are reaching for, making it undrinkable. This, in turn, only makes your thirst even more urgent. Thus caution and restraint are preferred, allowing you to sample the water to make certain that it is OK to drink as well as not to muck it up.

Happily, I must have played my role well because she asked me to join her, Bruce, and others the next morning before sunrise for breakfast. Like Muslims, the Bahai faithful observe the period of Ramadan (which is closely analogous to the Christian season of Lent). No eating is permitted during the daylight hours of each day. There is only breakfast and dinner; either before the sun rises or after it sets. I agreed to meet Vashti and the others for breakfast the next morning. I was truly interested in learning more about the Bahai faith. The more I learned about it, the more it seemed to be the answer to my recent questions and problems with, and prayers about Christianity.

In the weeks leading up to meeting these people, I had been contemplating that Jesus said that He was the waters of life, not the ice cube of life. Water is free and flowing, not frozen into a certain shape. I also knew that God is far larger and more dynamically complex than any one religion, Christianity included. I wondered why only following Christ through Christianity and not another path was reputed to be the only way to a new and improved life both here and, more problematically, for eternity.

Just west of Corvallis and the OSU campus, there is a small stream that flows out of the Coast Range, meanders across fields, then merges into a nearby river that itself flows east from a different area in the Coast Range. That river then flows into the Willamette River on the edge of downtown Corvallis. I knew the stream from many different places along its route, including its origin, as it flows through different fields and groves of trees. Along the way the stream grows in size and volume. The water is water all through its flowage but it takes on different characteristics and shapes according to varying locales and stream beds. It does not change in essence, it merely assumes the shape of its container which is the ever-changing stream bed.

Just as the stream changes shape and grows as it flows across the valley floor toward the nearby rivers, I wondered how the teachings of Jesus Christ might be freed from their current Christian context, whether musty, crusty Tradition or rigid, frigid Fundamentalism, so that the larger emerging global community could learn of and benefit from the teachings and Spirit of Jesus Christ.

Cultural Christianity is repulsive to me on either end of the spectrum. By this, I mean the complacent arrogance or vanity of thinking and acting superior to others because you know that you are saved, that you are right, and that you belong to the right church and say and do all the right things. It also produces stifling conformity out of fear of being wrong or different, which is to risk ostracism from your group. Of course, because this is a human flaw, spiritual arrogance, pride, and murderous conformity are not limited to just Christians. These corrupt attitudes and feelings allow and encourage some people to be cruel to other people in the Name of the Holy One while feeling good about it as if they are doing something brilliant, brave, and just. Every church and religion has them and the world suffers for it, but here I am only focusing on Christianity.

Within Christianity, spiritual arrogance, pride, and excessive conformity in thought, vocabulary, and personal appearance is a corruption of the true election, wringing the creatively radical out of it. The result is a cheap, empty facsimile of true love and true revelation, a second-hand religion instead of a daily reinspiration to new life and possibilities prompted by direct, ongoing experience of the Divine. I was bothered and angry that Christianity did not take on a fresh, new shape to accommodate our contemporary world and the convergence of cultures globally.

What I was learning about the Bahai faith seemed to be the answer to the direction that I thought I was being led by the Holy Spirit. The Bahai faith teaches the truth of one God, and also of one people, humanity. It also maintains that prophetic revelations of God are progressive, with our world being blessed by a series or line of prophets culminating in the savior who will appear and make all things right. I knew at the time that Jesus Christ was real and alive. I also believed that He will come again at some point in the future to judge the living and the dead and to establish a kingdom on a restored earth. Thus, I simply believed Jesus Christ would be the final prophet. In short, because of my ignorance about and selective inattention of certain key parts of the great Christian Tradition (the holy, apostolic faith once given for all that includes the holy scriptures); because of my disdain of much of current Christianity; and due to a desire to be comfortable intellectually and emotionally with the rest of the world in light of Jesus Christ, to not be secretly embarrassed about what appear to be prejudices or limits in Christianity, I was eager to learn more of the syncretistic Bahai faith. I remained confident that God was with me because I continued to feel His presence dwelling with me and in me.

In addition to seeking answers to my nagging spiritual questions, I was also very curious to know Vashti better. It seemed that she was possibly interested in me, as well. This excited me. Deeply, I was beginning to wonder if she was the woman whom I had dreamed of three or four weeks earlier. The next morning, I arrived at Vashti's house at about 6am, a half hour or so before sunrise. I could not believe my eyes! Vashti had tied her dark, black hair in a pony tail and bobby pinned it back up onto her head! I had already learned earlier that in the Bahai faith, people must receive permission to marry from both sets of parents, if living. I was 99% certain that she was the woman from the dream. I was filled with joy. God is so cool! He is blessing me with my heart's desires to be closer to Him apparently through the Bahai faith and to have a woman to love and cherish as a wife.

However, I did not indicate anything to Vashti or to the others present. I was still a little hesitant to believe what I thought was happening. I was still deciding whether God had ordained our relationship. I reasoned that if He had willed for Vashti to marry me, I would not have to try too hard to entice her into loving me —- that I should not force the situation. Sure enough, by the time breakfast ended that morning, it was clear that there was mutual attraction.

I had no reason to doubt that we were meant to be together for God had spoken to me through or in dreams a few times previously and those events came to pass. Yet, the dream of Vashti was unique for me. It was the first time ever that I had dreamed of someone before meeting them "here" in the "real" world. Dreams like that simply do not occur just for entertainment. Thus I accepted the dream and it's plot line very seriously, especially because it was now unfolding in this world exactly as it did in the dream. I had seen the script and was now playing my part in the movie. Over the next several weeks, our relationship not only sprouted, but began to put down roots, leaves formed, and flower buds appeared. I fell deeply in love with her but retained restraint in order to not scare her off. I also felt closer to God than ever before. Just because I knew how the movie ended did not mean that I should ruin it or force it for the other actors, namely Vashti.

At the same time that my relationship with Vashti was developing, I had to move out of the house that I had leased when I first arrived in Corvallis several months earlier because I had run out of money. However, I was confident that God would provide for me in one way or another. Afterall, He had so many times before, most recently with leasing the house in Corvallis and the manner in which the needed four roommates had appeared. There was also the incident on the Pacific Coast when I amazingly got the money and gasoline that I needed to get back to Corvallis (The Great Craftsman). I was not really worried, just concerned. It was also exciting because of the hoped-for Divine assistance. The deadline was February 1, 1980.

While waiting for the money details to work out, I swallowed hard and applied for food stamps because I had run out of money for food. It was a blow to my pride because I always prefer to work for my food than receive a "handout" but it was either food stamps or sifting through dumpsters. I wisely opted for the food stamps. Also, I was psyching myself up to either live out of my car for awhile or to establish a campsite somewhere in the beautiful Oregon countryside until I could afford to rent a place again.

For some reason, I stopped by the Global Studies Office to visit and to check again if anyone might know of any jobs. There were no new jobs that either Janet or Eric were aware of. While at the office, a woman named Marion called for Eric. She was a senior citizen who was Bahai. She had called Eric a couple of times previously to thank him for the Global Studies Office assisting in arranging the Bahai dinner and talk in January. Eric was too busy to take her call that day, so he passed her call to me. During the course of our conversation I must have made a joke about not having a place to stay. She offered to let me live in one of her unused bedrooms for the next several days while I waited for the Philomath Fire Department to make a decision regarding my application to be a sleeper. I immediately accepted her offer.

True to form, God had once again seamlessly provided for me. What an incredible, living God! Importantly, again, it seemed to me to be an indication of His approval of my emerging theological and spiritual direction regarding the need to update Christianity and my interest in the Bahai religion. If He did not like where I was growing, why would He clearly answer so many of my prayers regarding housing, food, a woman for a wife, and so forth? I was on the straight and narrow and it was a moving sidewalk. It was not that I was ramming prayers on God or that somebody else (evil) was answering them. I still enjoyed the privilege or gift of His presence. He was with me and all these wonderful things were happening for me in apparent direct response to my prayers to Him.

As it worked out, I only needed to stay with Marion for 10 days because not only was I accepted to be a sleeper at the Philomath Fire Department but the Department allowed me to move in right away instead of making me wait until March 1, 1980. I will always be grateful to Marion for her kindness. I know that she was a little lonely and I did help her a bit with some chores around her house, but it was I who benefited the most and I thank her for that. May God bless her.

I was now on salary from the universe, working for God. I was employed as a fireman and ambulance driver helping the community, I had a clean place to live, I had food (with enough spare change for gas money), I had new friends, I was in a relationship with a beautiful woman, my spiritual life was continuing to deepen and expand, and God seemed very close to me.

Coincidentally, Vashti lived in the small town of Philomath where the fire station was. I was now walking distance from her house, making it easier for our relationship to grow. As well, I was farther away from my family situation which allowed me to continue healing, becoming more myself. All of this on the western edge of the beautiful Coast Range in Oregon. All things considered, I was not doing too bad. I praised God greatly and often. Truly, 'all things do work together for the good of those who love God.'

While living at the fire station, a friend of one of the other sleepers invited me on a trip to Lake Tahoe for a few days. Clyde wanted to do a little gambling and his friend Jon, a fellow sleeper, was unable to get time off from his regular job at a local saw mill. Because I was still unemployed, I easily said, "Yes". Vashti and I said our good-byes, with the plan that we would get together the moment that I arrived back in town. While it was a good time to be with Clyde in Nevada and California, all I could really think about was Vashti. On our last day of the trip, Clyde and I visited the California side of the lake to try a specific casino Clyde knew of. I wandered through the gift shop while Clyde worked on getting winning card hands. I prayed for guidance in choosing a gift for Vashti. I saw a turnstile of earrings and walked over to it. I continued to pray while searching for a pair of earrings she might like. After only a minute or two, I selected a pair of antique brass earrings that had peacock feathers. They were very attractive.

Two days later it was Saturday morning. I was visiting Vashti, sitting at her kitchen table back in Philomath, Oregon. She was preparing coffee and bread for our breakfast. We were very happy to see each other again. Absence does make the heart grow fonder. That morning she was wearing a necklace that was quite striking. Various shapes and sizes of antique brass dangled from the brass rod neckband. She looked very beautiful, almost exotic, wearing it. I had never seen her wear it before. I was surprised because the earrings that I had bought in Lake Tahoe were perfectly matched to the necklace.

"That is a beautiful necklace you have on," I said.

"Thank you."

"I haven't seen you wear it before. Where did you get it?"

"It used to be my grandmother's. It has been passed down to me."

"It really is beautiful…you look beautiful wearing it. But do you have earrings that go with it?"

"No. For years, I have been looking for earrings that match this but I have not found any yet. I wish I had some."

With that response, I reached into my shirt pocket and retrieved the earrings, placing them on the table between us.

"Why don't you try these. I bought them for you in Lake Tahoe."

Her eyes popped wide open and her face lit up with surprise. My gift was a perfect match for the necklace as if the pieces were part of the same set. She picked the earrings up off the table and went to her bedroom to put them on. She returned a moment later, wearing them with the antique brass necklace. Both Vashti and I were amazed and happy. I believed that I sensed a deeper reality present as well: God. Truly it is very exciting when He answers prayer and blesses His faithful followers.

By late May or early June 1980, her family became alarmed that she might marry a non-Iranian who was also a couple years younger than her. They gave approval for an older, divorced Iranian entrepreneur who was a friend of the family from Los Angeles, California to begin romancing Vashti with intent to marry. Vashti did not like this development. With her parents stuck inside Iran due to the 1979 revolution, her brothers were the acting patriarchs. They lived in the Seattle-Bellevue metro area, less than 300 miles north of Philomath. Out of obedience to her family and culture, she began talking with this guy when he suddenly began calling on her. I was upset but trusted in my God to prevail. Vashti was to marry me as shown in my dream from January. The ongoing, powerful "coincidences" were independent confirmation of God's favor toward me. Only God can weave various threads of space-time into meaningful patterns such as answers to prayer, coincidences, and so forth. Besides, at that point, I had already edged out several other rivals for Vashti's affection. How much serious competition could this guy from LA give me?

One day in early June I took pita bread and halvah to her house. Earlier that day she had received a package from my competitor in LA. He too had sent my love pita bread and halvah! It seemed clear to me that I was being guided unconsciously by the Holy Spirit to defend the relationship that had been given to me. God and I were continuing to work together to affect His will that Vashti and I be married. On a different day that June, I picked a beautiful bouquet of wild field flowers and took them over to Vashti's house. We had talked earlier and I knew that she loved wild flowers as much as I did. I figured that it would be a nice

172

surprise for her. I knocked at her door and she let me in. There on her kitchen table sat a dozen white roses from Mr. LA. This guy was getting irritating. Both Vashti and I were stunned by the coincidence. After she moved his flowers off to the side and properly placed mine in the center of the table, we sat down for a cup of coffee.

"How come every time he sends me something, you give me the same thing the same day?" she asked.

"I don't know. I just know that I love you and that we are meant to be together. I know you better. I gave you your favorite halvah when he gave you a flavor you don't care much for. And now, he sends you white roses that you have said you dislike while I gave you flowers that I know you like," I said. I was doing my best to be the victor for her heart. It was a very odd moment.

She seemed a little scared by the coincidences. I felt uneasy too. It was great to have God on *my* side but it still seemed a little frightening or strange. I realized that if I told her about the dream, that might make her afraid of me and of our romance so I continued to keep it to myself. Perhaps someday I could tell her, but not at the moment.

As June became July, it was becoming ever more clear that I was losing Vashti, slowly but surely, to Mr. LA. Not that she was happy about it, but she was under great pressure to accept this man being promoted strongly by her family. One day in mid-July she walked out of her bedroom and shattered me, forever changing my life.

"I love you but I can't marry you. You are not Iranian, you are not Bahai, and you are younger than me."

We had never spoken about marriage although apparently we had both been thinking about it. I immediately gave her counterpoints, but she did not accept them, in part because it was clear to her that I was still too attached to Jesus Christ to be a good Bahai.

I had "converted" in a private meeting several weeks earlier at one of the local leader's homes. But the moment I did so, my spirit became very troubled deep inside. I felt terrible but tried to dismiss it, telling myself that I was just overly attached to Christianity. Within an hour, the conviction of having made a serious mistake became so strong that I felt like I was going to vomit or explode or something. I asked Christ for forgiveness. Within a few moments of my apology, I became calm. After that, I lost my enthusiasm for and interest in the Bahai faith. Yet for the sake of trying to maintain a relationship with Vashti, I was still going through the motions such as meeting her or other Bahais on campus to pray together. Maybe the two religions could coexist, I thought. However, when she told me that she could not marry me, I immediately dropped all pretense, especially with myself.

I knew that I was being dishonest with myself for the sake of preserving my faith, my understanding, my relationship with God, who He seemed to be, and how He works with us. Vashti and our relationship was a critical proof of my relationship with and approval by God. Thus, it was devastating to have the dream, all of the stunning coincidences, my somewhat improbable love affair with Vashti —- everything —- shattered by an unexpected and unpleasant ending. She married Mr. LA at the end of August 1980.

It hurt deeply to lose her to another guy but it hurt even more to lose the God that I thought I knew, the living God who seemed to love me so much. I was afraid of losing Him and of being lost if Vashti did not marry me. My structures of meaning were threatened. At first I was afraid that He really is too weak or too indifferent to have much impact on our daily lives. But then I let go of my illusions, my illusory hope. I felt like God had tricked me. I wondered if He was cruel and secretly enjoying my confusion and pain. However, within a couple of weeks I accepted that I must be wrong about God. The reason is that the true God must be 100% consistent and as logical as limited human understanding is capable of discerning. The situation no longer made any

sense. I reasoned that my understanding of who God is was inaccurate, that I did not really know who Jesus Christ was despite all the years of friendship and expanded reality experiences.
Why did He do this to me? He lead me on, He provided the coincidences, He seemed to approve my foray into creative new theology. I retreated into agnosticism and angry, rebellious hedonism while I tried to sort out my pain, anger, and confusion. It took nearly a year for my thoughts and feelings to cycle. During that time God did not abandon me although I usually felt distant from Him, estranged by a skittish wariness like a dog that has been abused. I just didn't know who He was and wasn't sure if I should trust Him again. I still did not accept the Christianity that we all usually see or experience, but I dared not go running after other things. I chose the relative empty safety of agnostic hedonism while I figured things out. All I knew for certain was that God had deliberately drawn out my icons of misunderstanding and misconception of who I thought He was and how He interacts with us, and He smashed them.

I understood immediately that Jesus Christ cannot be updated from the historic, orthodox Christian understanding as witnessed and recorded for all generations in the New Testament of the Bible and as affirmed by the early Church Councils. That person, that Jesus Christ, is the one that thousands of early Christians of the Roman Empire came to know and love. Nobody, definitely not thousands, in their right mind would willingly accept heinous discrimination, public shame, torture, and gruesome death for just a learned man or a prophet, specifically one who was not resurrected from death as a living person, who interacts with His people through the Holy Spirit. All the religions or personal fancies that have arisen since that time do not add any accuracy or truth to our knowledge of Jesus the Christ. It was a hard lesson to learn, but I am grateful God taught it.

Chapter 21
They are My People, too

One day during Fall Term 1979 at OSU, my cultural anthropology class viewed a film on certain subcultures around the world. I no longer remember the exact subject or purpose of the film. However, what I do remember is profound both in meaning as well as it's lasting impact on me.

A section of the film profiled "Holy Rollers", a Christian sect located in the Appalachian Mountains of West Virginia and eastern Kentucky. This sect interprets the Bible concretely, word for word. Thus, among other beliefs, they believe that they are empowered by the Holy Spirit to handle rattlesnakes without harm while dancing in trance-like states, often while speaking in tongues. They base this core belief of theirs on events in the New Testament, such as Luke 10, where Jesus empowered His followers to go out and preach the gospel and to handle poisonous snakes either without being bitten or at least without getting sick or dying from the snake bites.

To most people, even other Christians, their behavior seems foolish if not stupid. Christ died for our sins, not our minds. Common sense says that you should not play with poisonous snakes unless you are wearing protective gear and know what you are doing. Also, we are instructed in Holy Scripture to not tempt God by placing ourselves in unnecessary danger.

I have absolutely no doubt that God can do anything and that He is limited by nothing except perhaps respect for our free will as demanded by the love that He is. God is not limited by our imaginations or by our sensibilities or even by our common sense. He might enjoy the faith that the Holy Rollers express in Him as they dance about with live rattlesnakes, no matter how strange it might seem to most other people. However, God did endow humanity with abilities and skills, including common sense. Behaving contradictory to prudence on a regular basis, such as the Holy Rollers seem to do, is arguably not proper worship of God, nor a proper way to live.

Thus I shared an important, insightful, unsolicited opinion with Jesus during the film, out of my embarrassment as well as concern for His cause.

"See, that is why more people don't follow You. Look at those silly people. Who wants to act like that to follow You? It's not necessary in order to be close to You, yet this (mentally gesturing toward the movie screen) is what the world often thinks of when nonbelievers think of following You."

"They are My people too."

His rebuke was immediate and very present as if He were standing directly behind me. His voice was calm, clear, and unapologetic, the gentle firmness of complete authority. It was all that He said but that was all God needed to say. I felt like a jerk about one inch in height. I apologized quickly.

I suddenly began viewing the Holy Rollers as distant cousins in Christ, although I did not feel much kinship with them. To my surprise, Jesus apparently accepts anyone who trusts Him, including the "Holy Rollers", as much as He may enjoy me or other followers who have a different experience, understanding, and character (both individually and corporately) in His Spirit. It was also clear that Jesus does not worry whether the world might view Him or His people as being goofy or foolish.

Since that moment in the auditorium, I have grown to reserve judgment of others whom I might have snickered at before. His rebuke challenged me to respect all others who profess love for Him and trust Him even if those other people may irritate me or misunderstand me or judge me because I am not like them and do not belong to their church. For me to do otherwise is sin, to fall short of who I should be.

This is not to say that proper theology, clarity in faith, and rational thinking are not important. These are essential to a true or accurate faith. The point that I understood Jesus was teaching me is that complete trust and simplicity of faith in Him and the Holy Spirit, like a child's faith in her or his parents, is prized by God and makes all those who do so members of the same family. Everything else in every church, sect, and expression of Christianity, important though it may be, is secondary.

Chapter 22
Shasta & the Traffic

I have always loved dogs. I grew up with dogs in our house. Some of my best friends have been dogs. Thus I was pleased when my friend Rick asked me to "baby-sit" his dog, Shasta, for several hours one Spring weekend in 1981when I was living in Corvallis, Oregon. I knew Shasta from when she was a puppy two years earlier. The three of us had been on a couple of minor adventures together. Most often, we played catch in a nearby park. Shasta was as happy to hang out with me as I was to be with her. Shasta was also a good "chick magnet", a quality not to be overlooked. Almost everyone appreciates a beautiful Siberian husky with a sunny disposition.

On his way to attend to whatever he had to do that Saturday, Rick dropped Shasta off at my basement apartment. It is part of a grand old house located on the southern end of downtown Corvallis. Outside, it was a beautiful Spring day in the Willamette Valley, making it difficult to stay indoors. After a while, I decided to take Shasta outside for a short walk and to play. As soon as I attached the leash to her collar, Shasta began straining against it in the direction of the door. She did not need any coaxing up the steps to the empty, large, rectangular lot immediately behind the house. Bounded by parallel rows of houses on the two long sides with streets at either end of the shorter sides, the large, empty lot was a good place to take Shasta.

Like most any dog, despite how quickly I walked or followed her lead about the lot, she strained against her leash. We knew each other from many times together in the past, so I trusted Shasta enough to let her off the leash. The moment I did so, she immediately trotted away from me, following a meandering scent through the lot. I only looked away for just a moment.

When I looked back to where Shasta should have been, given

181

her previous speed and direction, she was not there. I scanned the area quickly only to see her on the north side of the lot 150 feet away from where I was. She was about to trot into the busy local city street. The first of a line of cars in the closest lane was beginning to nose-dive, braking suddenly. Cars in the far lane heading away from town were braking too. I felt sick and helpless in a flash. Instinctively I yelled her name.

"Shasta!"

Amazingly, Shasta literally pivoted 180 degrees without changing speed just like a weather vane, now heading straight back to me. Another two feet and the dog would have been either seriously injured or killed, that's how close it was.

I was astounded and relieved. As elation welled up inside me, the following resonated through my mind as clear as crystal.

"By your obedience you are saved."

It stunned me. That is all He said. His calm, strong, direct voice was a single thunderclap, interrupting the thoughts and feelings I had at the time. His words rumbled through me for several minutes, playing over and over in my mind. "To repent" literally means "to turn around." I knew this when He spoke to me. The combination of seeing the dog pivot like a weather vane and hearing the rebuke stunned me.

I put Shasta back on her leash, praised her for her obedience, and began to walk back towards my apartment. I knew what He meant: that I needed to stop rebelling out of anger and pain and to submit again to a relationship with Him.

Chapter 23

Journeying On My Path

It has been 30 years since I reached out to God in hopeful trust and He answered me as I walked through the moonlit fields behind my childhood home. Our relationship has grown from friendship into a deep, joyful love and knowledge of each other.

In reality, it is I who has grown and changed the most, becoming ever more capable and desirous to reflect back to Him and to the world the love and respect He freely gives me. I do this both directly through frequent thought and conversation with Him as well as trying to act with kindness, gentleness, patience, and love toward other people and in so far as possible, with our earthly biosphere. In the Gospel of Mark, one of the things the author wrote about Jesus is that He went about doing good. What a great habit of being to emulate. Although I am not always successful or willing in controlling my thoughts, feelings, and actions, frequently I am able to do so. As I work with the Holy Spirit over the years, I am learning and practicing to live indrawn, not outdrawn or withdrawn; to be balanced and poised like the center a spinning bicycle tire with my axis being Christ.

Like anyone else, I have some regrets about things I have done and things that I didn't do. Healing from my toxic family situation has been bittersweet at times because I could see lost opportunities that I could not or did not seize when presented with them. However, I am deeply appreciative of the wonderful life that I do have, that I have worked hard to help create. Wonderfully, in some strange, mysterious way, I seem to be exactly who and where I should be, as if God had anticipated all of the detours and slippage in my life to date, actually using them as part of the process of my becoming, just as an artist or sculptor uses every movement of their hand to create something unique, beautiful, and valuable.

Over the years I have come to accept and savor the mystery of questions, observations, and experiences not easily understood or that defy honest, definite answers; that is, a simple answer at the expense of truth. Our lives are permeated with mystery if we only pause a moment to listen to the fullness of the silence, to the dominant element of our existence. I accept the fact that Life is an unfathomable mystery more so than it is a neat collection of scientific facts, finite scripture verses, or specific experiences. Rather, I believe that the mysteries of Life are to be contemplated and wrestled with on the workbench of my daily experience. My faith must bridge the gap between the known and the unknowable, and it does through a loving trust in the Unseen God.

As I have become more tolerant and aware of mystery, and for the differences and similarities between people, I am ever more filled daily with awe and respect for life, for others, and for the Void From Whom All Things Come, God the Father. The longer I live, despite whatever suffering or pleasure I may be experiencing, life becomes more wonder-full. Life in union with God through His Holy Spirit has healed me; has made me strong; has cleansed me of anger and bitterness; has expanded my heart and mind; and has given me a great resiliency of spirit. No matter what happens, I know without doubt that I have come from God, I am walking with God, and that one day I shall return to God more fully to begin the next phase of my life. Nothing can separate me from His love. Knowing this gives me great joy and peace and freedom.

Like water
I have learned to flow around obstacles.

As the tree yields to the wind,
I know that I will
spring back from opposition.

Though fires may come,
I will
rise again, reborn
like the field grasses.

Like the spider and the hawk,
I see that all things
are connected.

Though the sun may be obscured by clouds,
it will shine again.
So too, will I.

Like the common weed,
I cannot be defeated.

Thanks be to God.

ABOUT THE AUTHOR

Mark lives in the Chicago, Illinois area with his wife and son. He earned a BA in Liberal Studies: Current Global Trends from Oregon State University in 1982, and an MBA in Finance from Keller Graduate School in 1993. This book is the result of his desire to know God and the challenge to understand expanded reality experiences in proper historical and cultural context. These interests require study of scripture, various theologies, religions, myths, and psychology. First and foremost, though, this fascination requires indulgence of the simple desire to love and be close to God. Currently he is at work on other books, short stories, and poems.